JEWISH ENCOUNTERS

Jewish Encounters is a collaboration between Schocken and
Nextbook, a project devoted to the promotion of Jewish literature, culture, and ideas.

>nextbook

PUBLISHED

Jews and Power

RUTH R. WISSE

JEWS AND POWER

NEXTBOOK · SCHOCKEN · NEW YORK

Schocken Books and colophon are registered trademarks of
Penguin Random House LLC.

Library of Congress Cataloging-in-Publication Data
Wisse, Ruth R.
Jews and power / Ruth R. Wisse
        p. cm. — (Jewish encounters)
Includes bibliographical references.
ISBN: 978-0-8052-1174-0 (paperback)
ISBN: 978-0-307-53313-5 (ebook)
    1. Jews—Politics and government.   2. Judaism and politics.
3. Jews—Identity.   4. Jews—Civilization.   5. Zionism.   I. Title.
    DS140.W57 2007   305.892'4—dc22   2006039228

Cover image: Disputation between Jewish and Christian
theologians/Lebrecht History/Bridgeman Images
Cover design by Kelly Blair

www.schocken.com
Printed in the United States of America
First Paperback Edition
2   4   6   8   9   7   5   3   1

For Neal Kozodoy

CONTENTS

INTRODUCTION TO
THE PAPERBACK EDITION

Much has happened in relations between Israel and other nations since the publication of this book in hardcover in 2007, but, unfortunately, nothing that renders its arguments obsolete.

Some of the news from the intervening years has been hopeful, though hardly all. Anti-Zionism is refueling anti-Semitism in parts of Europe even as some Arab and Muslim leaders consider ending the war against Israel that revved up anti-Zionism in the first place. Israel has made significant technological and diplomatic advances, has prospered economically, and consistently achieves high standing on the international index of happiness. Meanwhile, the regional surge in weaponry and aggressive rhetoric increases the real threat to its security.

However consequential, these contradictory developments have not altered the political patterns that I described in *Jews and Power*. Rather, they make it all the more important to understand why things happen as they do. For that purpose, I turn here to the most unexpected change of all, which has occurred not in the Middle East but in the United States.

In America, the "almost promised land," as Abraham Lincoln described it, Jews have long experienced unprecedented freedom both individually and as a people, have been encouraged to maintain their religious and ethnic particularity while uniting with fellow citizens in a cohesive polity. Correspondingly, popular support for Israel was strong enough in the latter decades of the twentieth century that candidates for national office from both parties would routinely tout their positive voting record on the Jewish state. As for American Jews themselves, they supported Israel as naturally as Greeks and Italians did their own homelands.

But darker currents were brewing. "No one pays any attention to the United Nations," a colleague assured me in late 1975, when the United Nations General Assembly stunningly passed Resolution 3379 declaring Zionism a form of racism. Yet far from being ignored, that resolution marked a turning point in the war against the Jews. Arab belligerents mobilized the Muslim–Soviet voting bloc to internationalize aggression against Israel under the aegis of the organization whose charter their own refusal to recognize or coexist with Israel had blatantly defied. Exchanging threat for accusation, they charged Israel with their own crimes. Having failed to "drive the Jews into the sea," they accused Jews of waging elimination warfare against Palestinian Arabs. Underappreciated at the time, this political repositioning made anti-Zionism palatable to Western and American elites.

Even when anti-Israel propaganda began to penetrate the universities, I was certain that Americans would withstand the assault. One example among others was particularly reassuring: an opinion piece in the summer of 1992 by Henry Lewis Gates, then chair of Harvard's Department of Afro-American Studies. In this essay, Gates warned against the rise of anti-Semitism among black Americans in particular, which he found most pronounced among the young and better educated. He said that blacks could not defeat anti-black racism in America if they practiced racism themselves.

Gates also described just how anti-Jewish politics worked. The followers of the Reverend Martin Luther King Jr. intended to normalize black politics by forging common cause with fellow Americans. But they were now being opposed by leaders who, increasingly linking themselves with Muslim militants, resorted to classic anti-Jewish tactics for a "barricaded withdrawal into racial authenticity," and were mobilizing animosity toward Jews to gain adherents. Gates spelled out the dangers of this "ethnic isolationism." European nationalists had used anti-Semitism the very same way.

He was equally incisive about the role of Jews. They might wonder how their political commitment to the civil rights struggle could have led to this situation. What they failed to realize was that the new anti-Semitism arose not in spite of the black–Jewish alliance but because of it. "Transracial cooperation—epitomized by the historic partnership between blacks and Jews—is what poses the greatest threat for the isolationist movement." The Jews' liberal drive for equal opportunity on a level playing field stood in the way of grievance politics. Jews needed accommodation; anti-Jews needed an object of blame.

Relieved, I took Gates's analysis as a sign that that the problem could be contained, but I could not have been more mistaken. What Gates disparaged as ethnic isolationism almost immediately turned respectable in the form of *identity politics*, and the movement he once feared might discredit African Americans now blended into a new consortium of grievance groups under the banner of "intersectionality." This spectacularly expanded the base. In the new century, anti-Zionism united radical and grievance factions just as anti-Semitism had done in Europe the century before. The speed of this development was not unprecedented, either; for the first time in America, the Arab war against Israel was taken up by elements in one of the two major political parties. An anti-Jewish position was no longer an automatic disqualification for public office.

Jews and Power explains how and why the Jews continue to serve as a political target whether dispersed or sovereign, militarily helpless or resolutely armed. I wish the book and its message had become obsolete over the past thirteen years, but instead they have gained urgency, including where least expected.

PROLOGUE

In Warsaw in the autumn of 1939, shortly after the Germans captured the city and before they had walled up the Jews in a ghetto, a couple of Nazi soldiers were seen harassing a Jewish child on the street. The child's mother ran out of the courtyard, picked up her bruised little boy, placed his cap back on his head, and said to him, "Come inside the courtyard and *za a mentsh*." The word *mensch*—which in German means "man" or "human being"—acquires in Yiddish the moral connotation of "what a human being ought to be." In her Polish-inflected Yiddish the mother was instructing her son to become a decent human being.[1]

Two years later in London, Shmuel (Samuel) Zygelboym described this incident to the Yiddish poet Itsik Manger. Manger had left Warsaw for Paris before the German invasion, intending to move on to Palestine, but once the war broke out, his ship was diverted and he was fortunate to make it to Liverpool, then to London. There he spent the rest of the war, haunted by the massacre that was overtaking his family back home. Zygelboym had been forced into the Warsaw Ghetto in November 1940 along with the rest of the city's Jewish population, but as a leader of the Jewish Socialist Bund he was smuggled out to England by members of his political movement to be their representative in the Polish government-in-exile. Zygelboym tried vainly to persuade Polish and Allied authorities to do whatever they could to help rescue Polish Jews who were being starved in the ghettos and exterminated in the death camps. When Manger later transcribed the Warsaw incident as Zygelboym had told it to him, he added that no other people on the darkening continent of Europe took as seriously as Jews did the injunction to be fully human.

What so impressed these men about the mother's instruction to her son was that rather than warn against his tormentors, she warned him not to become like them. Manger and Zygelboym ascribed great value to the mother's exact words, because although they no longer bothered to cover their heads, they felt that Yiddish had absorbed the moral values of Jewish religious civilization. The term *mentsh* conveyed to them the essence of Jewishness; they championed *mentshlekhkayt*—a commitment to human decency and mutual respect. Zygelboym took this a step further by adopting socialism as the new embodiment of Judaism for the modern age. *"Za a mentsh"* was thus the point at which these two modern Jews and the traditional mother still formed part of a common culture and could equally claim to be upholding the "golden chain" of Jewish values that ran from Abraham through Moses and the Hebrew Prophets to them.

I was raised in this same culture, studying Genesis alongside the poems of Itsik Manger. The Montreal Jewish school I attended drew no distinction between religion and nationality: Jewish values were transmitted as a passion for justice. We were expected to rescue the remnant of the Jews of Europe by helping to build a Jewish homeland in Palestine, as well as to improve Canadian society by good citizenship and good deeds. These teachings were reinforced by example in my home. Although my father had been decisively disabused of his Communist leanings when he was a university student in Poland, his greatest pride once he became a manufacturer was that his factory had never endured a strike. The Quebec labor leader who negotiated for the textile workers' union spoke admiringly of his decency and fairness. It was emphasized in my family, school, and community that far from granting us license, our laxity in the observance of Jewish ritual called for greater moral discipline in everyday affairs.

Need I say that I continue to honor this commitment to an ideal of social justice? Jewish moral idealism remains invaluable to the world for encouraging, despite much evidence to the contrary, faith in human potential of *mentsh* or its Hebrew equivalent, *ben-adam*, literally, "son of Adam" or "child of Man." I also understand why so many Jews join Manger and Zygelboym in seeking political or social ways of "repairing the world."

But my idea of human decency was also enlarged by something else that I learned in school when our principal addressed us in the auditorium about the carnage that had just taken place in Europe: "If each of you was to take a notebook and write on every line of every page the name of a different child, and if we collected all your notebooks, it still would not equal the number of Jewish boys and girls who were murdered by the Germans." On May 12, 1943, Shmuel Zygelboym had committed suicide in public protest against the Allies' indifference to the extermination of the Jews. This kind of information complicated the directive to be a *mentsh*. That little boy in Warsaw could not have done his mother's bidding, because becoming fully human presupposed staying alive. After most of its 380,000 Jews had been starved or deported to the Treblinka death camp and the Jewish resistance had launched its belated revolt, the Warsaw Ghetto was torched by the Germans, who then flushed out and killed the last pockets of Jews hiding in its attics and bunkers. Zygelboym's suicide acknowledged the political consequence of the moral solipsism he had admired four years earlier. The phrase *moral solipsism* describes a reckoning that is preoccupied with its own performance to the exclusion of everyone else's.

That mother in Warsaw could not have known what lay ahead of her and her child. German thinkers and scientists, artists and musicians, had earned for their country a reputation as the most cultured nation in Europe. The moderately decent behavior of conquering German soldiers in Poland in World War I gave little inkling of their murderous potential. The jurist Raphael Lemkin had to coin the term *genocide* in 1942 to describe the unprecedented systematic extermination of an entire national, racial, political, or ethnic group. By no fair standard can European Jews be blamed for having failed to *anticipate* German intentions. The same cannot be said, however, for those who come after the genocidal war against the Jews—what English calls the "Holocaust," Hebrew, the *Shoah*, and Yiddish, the *khurbn*—the same term it uses for the destruction of the Temple. The obligation to be decent is complicated for Jews by the knowledge that other societies feel driven to eliminate them from the world. Those who aspire to be decent human beings would be morally obtuse to the point of wickedness were they to retell Zygelboym's story without considering its outcome.

Political thinkers normally include national defense as part of their planning. Plato situates the soldiers of his Republic right below rulers: he assumes that the just society must protect itself against enemies. In its reach for a perfect Union, the Constitution of the United States undertakes to "establish justice, insure domestic tranquility, *provide for the common defense*, promote the general welfare, and secure the blessings of liberty to ourselves and our posterity" (my emphasis). Both Plato and the framers of the American Constitution thought it self-evident that their own nations might have to be defended. The Jews of Europe had no such provision or strategy for their common defense at the point when Hitler singled them out for extermination. Jews had concentrated on their moral improvement with no political structure in place to defend Jewish civilization or the children who were expected to perpetuate it.

T his book honors the memory of the Warsaw mother who wanted her son to become a *mentsh*, as well as the civilization that perpetuates her teaching. That teaching made Jews into the comeback kids of a saga that defies historical probability. The creation of Israel in the same decade as the destruction of European Jewry seems to me a more hopeful augury than the dove's reappearance to Noah with an olive leaf after the flood. President Mahmoud Ahmadinejad of Iran calls Israel a "rotten, dried tree that will be eliminated by one storm." I think not. Jews have lived to see the downfall of every Haman and Hitler. More likely, Ahmadinejad's words foretell the fate of a different desiccated society—his own.

And yet, Jews do seem to suffer from a political deficiency. Politics has been defined as the art or science of government or governing, especially the governing of a political entity, such as a nation. Though Jews have always constituted a nation, their political experience became the more exceptional the longer they flourished, and their atypical political patterns inspired the mistaken belief that they had no politics. This belief, in turn, prevented them and others from understanding their political interaction with other nations. To this day, Jews figure more prominently in the study of religion than they do in the study of government or political theory. Political science has shown little interest in a nation that doesn't fit its paradigms.

To address this deficiency as I see it, this book highlights the political aspect of Jewish experience. In particular, I want to see how the politics of Jews occasions the politics of anti-Jews. I look at the politics of Jews and anti-Jews in tandem because that is the way they coexist. Some readers may be concerned that such linkage would appear to hold Jews responsible for the aggression leveled against them. Rather, the tendency of Jews to seek fault in themselves is part of the harmful pattern I hope to expose. Psychologists do not demean their patients by inquiring into the patterns of abuse they have sustained. Neither should our inquiry into the patterns of Jewish political strategy be mistaken for reproach.

How did the Jews get to figure so prominently in the political sights of precisely those regimes that threaten the rest of the world? Why does the president of Iran feel entitled to call for the destruction of a member nation of the world organization that presumably secures their equal rights? Democracies, if they are to remain democratic, know they must come in on the side of the Jews, but why is it so hard for them to recognize that it is in their interest to do so? How and why did anti-Semitism become arguably the most protean force in international politics? To paraphrase the rabbis, the inquiry is not ours to finish, but neither are we free to desist from it.

Jews and Power

PART ONE

The Great Experiment

There was no one left for the soldiers to kill or plunder, not a soul on which to vent their fury; for mercy would never have made them keep their hands off anyone if action was possible. So Caesar now ordered them to raze the whole City and Sanctuary to the ground, leaving the towers that overtopped the others . . . and the stretch of wall enclosing the City on the west—the wall to serve as protection for the garrison that was to be left, the towers to show later generations what a proud and mighty city had been humbled by the gallant sons of Rome. All the rest of the fortifications encircling the City were so completely leveled with the ground that no one visiting the spot would believe it had once been inhabited. This then was the end to which the mad folly of revolutionaries brought Jerusalem, a magnificent city renowned to the ends of the earth.[1]

JOSEPHUS, *The Jewish War*

The loss of Jewish sovereignty was the defining political event in the life of the Jewish people. Before then, Judea with its capital Jerusalem had been a province of the Roman Empire, paying heavy tribute to Rome yet conducting its affairs with perceived, if not complete, autonomy. Despite intense discord among Judea's religious and political factions, King Herod had restored the splendor of the Temple, which served as the center of legislative and religious activity. But the capriciousness of Roman rule angered many Jews and provoked them to armed revolt. In 70 CE, following a three-year siege, Titus crushed the Jewish uprising and burned the Temple, leveling the city—as Josephus describes, so that "no one visiting the spot would believe it had once been inhabited." Sixty-five years later, Rome put down a second Jewish rebellion with a brutality that deterred all further insurrection. Though some Jews always continued to live in the Land of Israel, the vast majority over the next eighteen centuries tried to follow the Jewish way of life outside its borders.

Memory of the national defeat seemed to divide Jewish history into unequal parts: the relatively shorter span when Jews had inhabited their land and the longer stretch of exile when they were ruled elsewhere by others. Mourning the Great Destruction became so intense that it almost rivals praise of God as the central motif of Jewish worship. "Rebuild Jerusalem the holy city quickly in our time," reads the liturgy incorporated into the grace after meals. Every Jewish ceremony and celebration invoked the Great Destruction and expectation of Return. When a Jew dies, family members are consoled with the words, "May God comfort you among the other mourners of Zion and Jerusalem." For three weeks of every year, culminating in the fast of the ninth day of the Hebrew month of Av, Jews commemorate the fall of Jerusalem. The annual Passover Seder concludes with the pledge, "Next year in Jerusalem."

When modern Jewish thinkers began to study the Jewish past, they, too, divided history into before and after. The great historian Heinrich Graetz (1817–1891) separated the "predominantly political character" of the pre-exilic period from the "overriding religious stamp" of the exile. That Graetz was the first Jewish historian since Josephus to attempt to tell the complete story of the nation seemed to substantiate his argument that Jews had lost their political character at the point of going into exile. According to Graetz, Judaism was originally not a religion at all but "a constitution for a body politic": the idea of God was originally meant to work itself out not theologically but in the living history of the Jewish people. Only after the exile did religious interests gain exclusive control so that "Judaism ceased to be the constitution for a state and became a religion in the usual sense of the word."[2] Taking politics to mean that which concerns the state and its institutions, historians following Graetz assumed that with the dispersion, Jews had ceased to function as a political people.

Not all Jewish scholars and historians shared Graetz's regret for the consequences of the exile. Some modern thinkers became convinced that despite its liabilities, the absence of political power had benefited the Jewish people in the long run. Herman Cohen, the main spokesman for liberal Judaism in Germany in the early years of the twentieth century, held that Jews had been able to develop a universal ideal of messianic redemption because they had been freed of the *burdens* of a state. In his view, Jewish religion alone was the driving force of modern Jewish life, having become more ethically advanced because it was freed of nationalism and a state apparatus. "Religion ought to become more political by educating citizens in the love of humanity, while politics ought to assume the religious tasks of mediating between the individual and the rest of humanity." Purified of the dross of politics, no longer bound by their own territory, Diaspora Jews could become better citizens of the countries in which they lived.[3] Immanuel Kant's ethical ideals could be realized more fully by Jews than they could by Christians precisely because Jews were unscathed by the corruptions of power.

The Russian Jewish historian Simon Dubnow, Cohen's ideological opposite in all other respects, agreed that as a consequence of exile Jews had become a spiritual nation, purified, reborn for new life.[4] Jews were for him primarily a nationality, not a religious group. Encouraged by the model of a multiethnic Austro-Hungarian empire, he believed that Jews were already ahead of the curve in transcending the grosser demands of statehood. "A nationality which lacks a defensive protection of state or territory develops, instead, forces of inner defense and employs its national energy to strengthen the social and spiritual factors for unity."⁵ Locating Jewish strength precisely where materialists would have sought its weakness, Dubnow believed with Cohen that Jews could claim preeminence in the modern world not in spite of but on account of their lack of political power. He expected Jews to remain strong national minorities wherever they lived in sufficient numbers, maintaining their national distinctiveness through language, culture, education, and social institutions. His most radical proposal was that the kahal, the medieval Jewish community council, could be reconstituted as a secular institution of Jewish autonomy as part of a federated European state.

Dubnow's hopes for Jewish minority status in Europe were sorely tested by his own experience; he was forced to flee from St. Petersburg to Berlin after the collapse of the tsarist empire, then from Berlin to Riga after the rise of Nazism, and was driven to his death from the Riga Ghetto on December 8, 1941. It would be unfair to say that he paid the price for his optimism, since the Germans arranged the same ending for all Jews, irrespective of the ideas they had held. But some of his fellow intellectuals had been warier of establishing a politically viable autonomy in Europe, warning that Jews must first be granted their natural rights as Jews, not merely as citizens, as a precondition for their national recovery. In 1873 the Yiddish and Hebrew novelist known by the pen name of Mendele the Book Peddler (Mendele Moykher Sforim) had described a pack of dogs and a gang of boys beating an old mare to the point of death. When the bloodied creature is discovered in the ditch— behold! She speaks, claiming to be of noble birth, transformed centuries ago by the sorcerers of Pharaoh into her present lowlier state. Briefly restored to human (and male) form by the Wonder Worker who led her out of Egypt, she was forced back into servitude by her enemies and kept in that servile condition for "as long as the Jewish exile." The Wandering Mare of this allegory reveals to her modern Jewish inter-locutor that she will be able to regain human form only if she is released from her curse by the (Gentile) powers that damned her.

Others reformers went further: in response to Russian pogroms of 1881, Leo Pinsker issued a call for Jewish self-emancipation, arguing that exile had turned Jews into a nation of zombies. Wandering like corpses among the living, they frightened Gentiles, who were afraid of ghosts.[6] The Hebrew poet Haim Nahman Bialik excoriated his fellow Jews for allowing themselves to become the targets of slaughter:

> Upon the mound lie two, and both are headless—
> A Jew and his dog.
> The self-same axe struck both, and both were flung
> Unto the self-same heap where swine seek dung.[7]

Wasting no sympathy on the victims, Bialik ignored instances of Jewish self-defense in order to magnify his indictment of Jewish submissiveness. Self-liberation became a watchword for those in the Diaspora who were determined to chart their own future.

Yet, sharply divided as all these Jewish intellectuals were on the Diaspora's benefits or liabilities, they mostly agreed that the departure from the Land of Israel had brought about a suspension of Jewish politics. Jewish political history was thought to have ended with the destruction of the Second Temple and started up again in the late nineteenth century. "We didn't make our own history, the *goyim* made it for us," declares Yudka, one of the best-known characters of modern Hebrew fiction, founding member of an Israeli kibbutz. Yudka would simply forbid teaching Israeli youngsters about a "collection of wounded, hunted, groaning and wailing wretches, always begging for mercy."[8] His is the extreme voice of pioneering Israel that, having left the Diaspora in body, also wished to repudiate its qualities of mind and spirit.

Not until the early 1970s—several decades after the establishment of the state of Israel—was there any serious challenge to this idea that Jews in the Diaspora had existed in a political vacuum. By that time, the concept of politics, once limited to that which concerns the state and its institutions, had broadened to include other manifestations of power. A number of scholars, among them several American immigrants to Israel, began studying the record of Jewish self-government with a view to uncovering its political traditions. They recognized that the absence of full sovereignty never meant that Jews had lacked political institutions or leaders. Rather, Jewish political traditions, grounded in the covenant (*brit*) with the Almighty, had generated an unbroken record of legal interpretation based on the reciprocity of relationship between the ruler and the ruled.[9] Some of these scholars traced modern political phenomena back to their biblical and post-biblical sources, while others teased out major trends of Jewish political thought and practice from rabbinic and philosophical literature. In place of the "absent" political dimension, researchers began to delineate features of Jewish political life that anticipated many features of liberal democracy, such as the rule of law, emphasis on individual rights and responsibilities, elected authority, and universal education.

This book takes for granted that Jews remained as politically active outside the Land of Israel as they had been within their own territory. In fact, I posit that Jewish creativity expressed itself no less in political adjustment to the Diaspora than in other realms of mind and spirit—and that Jewish politics is no less worthy of serious study than Jewish religion, philosophy, folkways, or culture. Moreover, since Jews everywhere interacted with other peoples and rulers, their politics played a critical role in international affairs. Other aspects of Jewish history may concern the Jews primarily; Jewish politics affected much of the world.

The Jewish Diaspora

The Jewish Diaspora is one of history's boldest political experiments, an experiment as novel as the idea of monotheism itself, and inconceivable without it. When the Romans devastated Jerusalem and sacked the Second Temple in 70 CE—Josephus cites 1.1 million Jewish dead—many Jews were forcibly taken to Europe as slaves. Though Jewish communal life continued in the Land of Israel, the majority of Jews began to cluster elsewhere, creating an ever-expanding network of small and larger settlements in Europe, North Africa, and Asia. Jews did not consciously plan to continue their national life outside the Land of Israel; neither, until modern times, did any of them develop an ideology committed to stateless existence. Yet to live abroad meant to thrive as a nation without three staples of nationhood: land, a central government, and a means of self-defense.

A blueprint for national life outside the Land of Israel had emerged much earlier, very soon after the formation of the original Jewish commonwealth. The Bible describes the seventy years during which David and Solomon ruled a united Israel (c. 1000–922 BCE) as a time of great cultural and material accomplishment. David is the Bible's darling—friend and lover, warrior and psalmist, the shepherd boy worthy of ruling a kingdom. His son Solomon is singled out in traditional sources as the "wisest of all men" and most successful of monarchs. Solomon's original Temple in Jerusalem radiates the spiritual and political authority of his reign.[10] Soon after Solomon's death, however, the country split into northern and southern kingdoms: Northern Israel disappeared with the fall of Samaria in 721 BCE; southern Judah warded off enemies for another 135 years but then fell to the Babylonians. The invaders destroyed the Temple that had served as the center of Jewish religious worship, and drove the Jewish leadership into exile. At that point the Jews might have evaporated in history, like so many another conquered people, leaving traces only in the ruins and inscription of their names on ancient tablets.

That they did not assimilate is largely a function of how they understood their relation to God. Through the covenant at Sinai, Jews had undertaken to serve an Almighty whose moral law curbed certain forms of behavior and required others. They had been promised that in return for obeying His law, they would someday multiply and prosper in their own country. "King of kings" was no mere metaphor but a precise description of how the Almighty dominated the political triangle that Jews thought they formed with foreign nations. Jews would be protected from aggressors if they satisfied the terms of their covenant with the Omnipotent. God would be the guarantor of Jewish power as long as Jews obeyed His laws.

Thanks to this understanding of their situation, the prophets felt justified in construing the defeat of the Jews as the consequence of God's dissatisfaction with His people.

The prophets taught that the political fate of the Jews depended on their ability to convince not their rivals of their military prowess, but God of their uprightness. They linked a nation's potency to its moral strength, putting the Jews on perpetual trial for their political actions before a supreme judge. By thus maintaining an independent reckoning, Jews did not have to accept conquest by their enemies as a judgment on their staying power. The same prophets who decried the sins that had caused the destruction of the Temple foretold that Jews would be restored to Zion once they repudiated idolatry and won back God's favor.

The explanation of military defeat as the consequence not of the enemy's prowess but of the Jews' failure to please the Lord insulated Jews from some of the vagaries of war. Jews obviously recognized the difference between conquest and being conquered, but by situating their politics within a transcendent scheme of judgment, they did not have to accept the verdict of the battlefield. A temporary rout left open the possibility for an eventual reversal, just as temporary displacement from the Land of Israel allowed for eventual return to it. The more power Jews ascribed to God, the more politically independent they became of the power other nations wielded over them. At the same time, a God who kept an extended rather than a short-term accounting instilled a sense of accountability that transcended the individual. The behavior of the entire people, their everyday habits, would determine the severity of collective punishment or the possibility of collective reward.

It is interesting to compare this concept of national service with the political nature of Christianity, which traces its origins to Judaism. By universalizing the teachings of the "holy people," Christianity escaped what it considered the ethnocentricity of the Jews. Israel's prophet Jeremiah calls on God to avenge His people: "Pour out Thy fury upon the heathen, and upon the families that call not on Thy name: for they have eaten up Jacob, and devoured him, and consumed him, and have made his habitation desolate."[11] Jesus according to Matthew preached just the opposite, saying, "You have heard that it was said, 'You shall love your neighbor and hate your enemy.' But I say to you, Love your enemies and pray for those who persecute you, so that you may be children of your Father in heaven."[12] Yet in due course, the universal church made common cause with the politically ambitious state, encouraging Christians to engage in national wars of conquest in order to spread their redemptive idea. One practical result of Christianity's catholic largesse was to release its adherents from *political* constraints. The most consequential of all its differences from Judaism was that it did not require a nation to adopt the religious standards of an individual. Christian countries may have fought in the name of God, but they did not contemplate fighting by the rules of their savior. This may help to account for the otherwise astonishing discrepancy between the teachings of Jesus and the brutality of so many rulers acting in his name.

Islam's relation to power is more direct than Christianity's, since the prophet Muhammad was himself a warrior and the description of his military exploits in the form of commentaries and commandments forms the basis of the Koran. Muhammad lived by the sword and never dreamed of beating it into a ploughshare. The Arab prophet imposed his religion through holy war, engendering no hesitancy about Islam's use of power as a corollary of its moral purpose. The historian Bernard Lewis points out that this difference between Islam and its sister religions goes back to the beginnings of Islam and the career of its founder.

> Unlike Moses, Muhammad lived to enter and conquer his promised land. Unlike Jesus, he triumphed in his lifetime over his worldly enemies and established an Islamic state in Medina of which he was sovereign. . . . Muhammad exercised the normal functions of a head of state—he dispensed justice, he raised taxes, he promulgated laws, he made war, he made peace. In other words, from the very beginning, in the sacred biography of its Prophet, in its earliest history enshrined in scripture and tradition, Islam as a religion has been associated with the exercise of power.[13]

Judaism's much more ambiguous relation to power likewise goes back to its earliest recorded history. Psalm 137 conveys the predicament of the captives in Babylon following the sack of Jerusalem. Their captors taunt the Jews by ordering them to perform "songs of Zion." The Jews refuse, uttering instead the pledge that will resound through the ages:

> If I forget you, O Jerusalem,
>> let my right hand wither;
>> let my tongue stick to my palate
>> if I cease to think of you,
>> if I do not keep Jerusalem in memory
>> even at my happiest hour.

When the Jews finally *do* "sing out" in that psalm, their tune is very different from the dirges that their captors demanded:

> Remember, O Lord, against the Edomites
>> the day of Jerusalem's fall;
>> how they cried, "Strip her, strip her
>> to her very foundations!"
> Fair Babylon, you predator,
>> a blessing on him who repays you in kind
>> what you have inflicted on us;
>> a blessing on him who seizes your babies
>> and dashes them against the rocks![14]

"Edomites" are the generic enemies of Israel, Babylon the immediate aggressor. Rather than crushing the Jews' morale, the scorn of their captors has spiked Jewish anger and stiffened national resolve.

The psalm's grisly pledge of retribution (a term some

scholars prefer to "vengeance") offended those readers of the Bible who had no stake in the political rehabilitation of the Jews. The Christian philosopher Augustine read Psalm 137 as an allegorical depiction of the victory over lust, the waters of Babylon representing "all things which here are loved and pass away"; the babies dashed against the rocks, "evil desires at their birth"; and Jerusalem, the condition of holiness rather than the Jewish homeland.[15] For their part, Jews fully intended to recover the land, allegorizing the term "Babylon" to include subsequent enemies of Israel. Almost 2,500 years after the Babylonian exile, at the end of the Second World War, a Jewish scholar expressed resentment that "non-Jewish critics, writing in comfort and security, usually deplore the bitter vindictiveness of the imprecation which ends the [137th] Psalm": He believed that Jewish refugees of Hitler's massacre would share the mood of the psalmist when they returned to their native cities that had been decimated by the Germans.[16]

Yet for all its rhetorical severity, Psalm 137 does not exhort Jews to take up arms on their own behalf. Assuming full moral responsibility for the violence that war requires, it calls on the Lord to avenge the Jews' defeat and on other nations to repay Babylon "in kind." This reflects the historical record: It was the Persians, not the Jews, who defeated the Babylonians, and King Cyrus who allowed the Jews to return to Jerusalem and to rebuild their Temple, thereby inspiring Isaiah's reference to him as "the Lord's anointed," the messenger of God's will. God's hand, not the soldiering of Israel, is credited with the Jews' political recovery, for had the Persians not prevailed and acted magnanimously, who knows how much longer it would have taken the Jews to return to their home?

The first Babylonian exile proved that the Jewish nation could survive outside the Land of Israel, leaving open the question of when and how they would regain it. Jews considered themselves actors in political history even when they lacked the power to shape it. From earliest days, Jewish sources distinguished "good" nations from "evil" according to whether they could tolerate Jewish distinctiveness.

Interpreting Catastrophe

The first period of Jewish exile after the fall of Solomon's Temple lasted fifty years, until the Persians, who had by then defeated the Babylonians, allowed the Jews to return to the Land of Israel and to restore their religious institutions. Word went down through subsequent generations that, thanks to the power of their monotheistic faith, the people's "inner strength had remained undiminished" despite the destruction of their national and territorial base.[17] If anything, the memory of defeat may have strengthened Jewish faith in historical reversal. Had they thought that it had tarnished their reputation, Jews would not have included the memory of enslavement so prominently in their liturgy and national remembrance.

During the Second Jewish Commonwealth, from 516 BCE to 70 CE, Jews rebuilt the Temple and resumed their way of life under a succession of regional overlords. Against the Hellenizing forces of Antiochus IV Epiphanes (175–163 BCE), the Maccabees spearheaded what has been called the first religious war in history.[18] Their victory is commemorated by the overtly national Jewish festival of Hanukah. Historians who otherwise differ in their appraisal of Jewish militarism are agreed that the Jews in ancient days fought hard for the right to govern themselves in their country. Roman sources confirm that seven decades after the sack of Jerusalem, Jewish revolts in Palestine still constituted the most serious military threats anywhere in the empire.[19] The Jews fought tenaciously and sometimes victoriously, and their defeats were correspondingly severe.

The only contemporary Jewish account of the fall of Jerusalem was written by the canny governor of Galilee, who switched sides during the conflict, defected to the Romans, and took the name Flavius Josephus. Josephus participated in the events that he describes in *The Jewish War*, the very title of which (echoing "The Punic Wars," "The Gallic Wars") advertises that it is being written from the perspective of the conquering Romans. Josephus did not apologize for his treachery. On the contrary, he justified his actions on the grounds that the Jewish fighters should never have taken up arms against Rome in the first place. Given his approach—summed up by one of his translators as "everything that Josephus did was right; anything that John or

Simon did was wrong"[20]—we should not be surprised that he blamed the Jews and vindicated the Caesar whose protection he had sought:

> I will state the facts accurately and impartially. At the same time the language in which I record the events will reflect my own feelings and emotions; for I must permit myself to bewail my country's tragedy. She was destroyed by internal dissentions, and the Romans who so unwillingly set fire to the Temple were brought in by the Jews' self-appointed rulers, as Titus Caesar, the Temple's destroyer, has testified. For throughout the war he pitied the common people, who were helpless against the partisans; and over and over again he delayed the capture of the city and prolonged the siege in the hope that the ringleaders would submit.[21]

Having joined the enemy, Josephus blamed the destruction on the "mad folly" of the Jewish zealots. That Josephus was a Jew seemed to credit the sincerity of his account.

Is it not curious that the destruction of the Second Jewish Commonwealth came to be known from the perspective of a Jew determined to vindicate its destroyer? Josephus became an esteemed emissary to the Gentiles, the interpreter of the Jews to others as well as to themselves. Jews not only lost the war against Rome, but they supplied the historian who held them responsible for their downfall. By the middle of the sixteenth century, Josephus had been translated into every major western European language. Gentiles and Christians among whom the Jews resided learned from him that the Jews had deserved their ruin.

One might have expected rabbinic commentary on the great destruction to offset Josephus's condemnation of the Jews. But the rabbis had reasons of their own for blaming the debacle on internal rather than foreign agencies. The Talmud's discussion opens with the curious case of Kamtza and Bar Kamtza, names likened by one scholar to Tweedledum and Tweedledee and obviously destined to be confused:[22] A certain Jerusalemite who had a friend named Kamtza and an enemy named Bar Kamtza once arranged a banquet, but the invitation that he sent to the first was accidentally delivered to the second. When Bar Kamtza showed up expecting to be welcomed at the feast, the host tried to evict the unwelcome guest from his home. Shame was at stake in being forced to leave. For the right to stay, Bar Kamtza offered to pay, first for his meal, then for half and finally for the entire banquet—but to no avail. Ejected, he held the sages who were present, along with the host, responsible for his humiliation and took his revenge by arousing Roman suspicions that the Jews were fomenting rebellion against them.

This is how the Talmud describes his actions:

Bar Kamtza urged Caesar to test the loyalty of the Jews by sending them an offering for their Temple to see whether they accept it. Caesar sent a perfectly fine calf, but on the way Bar Kamtza inflicted a blemish on the animal which made it ritually impure, hence against religious law to offer as a sacrifice. The sages were inclined to offer it in order to maintain peace with the government. But Rabbi Zechariah ben Avkulas protested, "People will say that blemished animals have been offered on the altar." Then it was proposed to have Bar Kamtza assassinated, so that he would not continue to inform against them. Again Rabbi Zechariah ben Avkulas demurred: "Is one who makes a blemish on consecrated animals to be put to death?" (Rabbi Yochanan was to remark: The scrupulousness of Rabbi Zechariah ben Avkulas, as well as his forbearance, destroyed our holy house, burned our Temple Hall, and caused us to be exiled from our Land.)[23]

With the inexorable logic of the children's poem, "For want of a nail the kingdom was lost," the Talmud describes how a misdirected invitation and a host's insult to his guest induced the villainy of Bar Kamtza, which then did its damage thanks to the overscrupulous legalism of Rabbi Zechariah. The rabbis recognized that as a subject minority, Jews were vulnerable to betrayal by their least satisfied members, who might be seeking revenge for real or imagined slights.

Compressed in this episode is an entire political treatise, but it is political thinking of a peculiar kind. Whatever their disagreements on the merits of the Jewish struggle against Rome, the rabbis directed their attention away from the details of war to the kind of political discipline that was required for prolonged life in other peoples' lands. "Kamtza and Bar Kamtza" became a byword for *sinat khinam*—hatred without rightful cause—that was said to have caused the downfall of the state. Why was the Second Temple destroyed? Because the Jews were rent by dissention.[24] To be sure, the implicit idea behind this explanation was that *the Romans were able to conquer the city* because the Jews were rent by internal dissention, but the Talmud subordinates Rome's function to the actions of the Jews and looks for explanations in Jewish rather than Roman behavior. Even Rabbi Yochanan, who ascribes defeat to the failure of Jewish realpolitik, thereby locates the error in his fellow Jews. The very nature of Talmudic debate turns the political focus inward, away from the enemy and toward its own constituency.

Thus, in differing ways and for dissimilar ends, Josephus and the rabbis both held their fellow Jews accountable for their political failure. Crediting defeat to their own mistakes rather than to the superiority of their assailants was a way of preserving moral independence, since it ascribed agency to Jews or to God rather than to the victors. Neither Josephus nor the rabbis railed against Roman imperialism or calculated how the Jews had been outmatched. In this sense, they reversed the politically "normal" accounts we find in the Hebrew Bible in which the nation prides itself on its military heroes and keeps score against its enemies. Adjustment to dependency in other people's lands educed a political narrative in which Jews retained control over their national destiny by accepting responsibility for their political failure.

The attribution of Jewish defeat to internecine warfare was itself a consequence of the Jews' defeat at the hands of Rome. In a cyclical pattern, adjustment to exile reinforced the habits of self-accountability, which permitted adjustment to exile. This triangulated view of politics was expected to bring about an eventual recovery of the homeland, just as had happened after the Babylonian exile. Every Jewish schoolchild learned that a gnat lodged in the brain of Titus Caesar drove to madness the man who had destroyed the Temple and paraded its treasures through the streets of Rome. Jews expected God to wreak His vengeance against their destroyers and to grant them victory whenever they proved themselves worthy of His trust. In what follows, we shall see how this response to conquest made possible a unique political adjustment to Diaspora. For the moment it is enough to recognize that no other people developed a similar long-range strategy of accommodation to defeat.

Adaptation to Extended Exile

The Roman emperor Hadrian renamed the Land of Israel *Syria Palestina*, or Palestine, to erase its connection to the Jews. Although Jews continued to inhabit the Land of Israel, and to call it just that, Eretz Israel, no second Cyrus ever conceded their native rights to that territory. Thanks to the earlier example of Babylonian captivity and institutions that encouraged decentralized authority, the rabbis could envisage prolonged sojourn in foreign lands. It only remained to develop the institutions that could sustain this political vision in everyday life.

By the time the Romans crushed the last Jewish revolt, Jewish society had undergone changes that eased its transition to life in exile. Chief among these was the nature of public worship. Rededication of the Temple may have been uppermost in the minds of the Jewish leadership that returned to Jerusalem from their Babylonian captivity in the middle of the fifth century BCE, but Jewish tradition singles out the achievement of Ezra the Scribe, who edited the Torah and placed its reading at the center of the national religion.

> On the first day of the seventh month, Ezra the priest brought the Teaching before the congregation, men and women and all who could listen with understanding. He read from it, facing the square before the Water Gate, from the first light until midday, to the men and women and those who could understand; the ears of all the people were given to the scroll of the Teaching.[25]

Ezra insisted that the scriptures be read aloud to the assembly and interpreted in the Aramaic vernacular. The Levites, or teachers, were to see to it that every man, woman, and sentient child not only heard but *understood* the national books. The same custom of reading and interpreting the Bible also spread to houses of prayer far removed from the Temple, ensuring that the foundational texts became the permanent Jewish core curriculum.

Because not all Jews had returned from Babylon when permitted to do so, Jewish life already flourished outside the Land of Israel during the period of Israel's sovereignty. There emerged a class of rabbinic scholars and interpreters whose court of law or Sanhedrin made its decisions binding on communities abroad. Once the rabbis began to codify the oral law that interpreted the biblical injunctions, they laid the groundwork for an independent judiciary with far-reaching powers in all areas of life. This judiciary was situated in Jerusalem, but it could also be situated elsewhere, teaching as it did that the world is sustained by three things—by the Torah, by worship, and by deeds of loving kindness—all of which could be observed outside the Land of Israel.[26] Synagogues, as yet more concentrated on study than prayer, sprang up within and outside the land, adumbrating the practice of Jewish religion through the later centuries. Jews learned to feel "at home while abroad" by refashioning institutions and practices once associated with the great Temple.[27]

The first-century sage Yohanan ben Zakkai is popularly credited with having allowed Judaism to survive the fall of Jerusalem, and his career illustrates the political adjustments that were necessary for an extended exile. Ben Zakkai was the youngest and most distinguished disciple of Rabbi

Hillel, who advocated study of the Torah and the promotion of its observances as the surest means of maintaining Jewish religious autonomy under Rome. In the sectarian conflicts of those years, Ben Zakkai was a member of the peace faction that warned against the fatal consequences of an all-out revolt against Roman rule. We do not know for certain whether he was a pacifist from the outset or joined the peace faction only once he became convinced that the Zealots could not defeat the Roman legions, but we do know that he left the city before its destruction (according to legend, smuggled out in a coffin) and persuaded the Roman commander Vespasian to allow him and his fellow rabbis to set up a center of study outside Jerusalem. Though he was not, like Josephus, joining the enemy, he acquiesced to defeat in order to get beyond it, and perhaps the coffin story is there to suggest that he died as one kind of Jew in order to reemerge as another.

Whether the Romans sent Ben Zakkai to Yavneh (Jamnia) because it was one of their cities of detention or whether he chose it because it already had a functioning Beth Din, or Jewish judicial court, this "clear-eyed realist" took the first steps to reconstitute Jewish religious and political authority outside the Land of Israel. By getting permission from the Romans to found an academy abroad, he became the nation's guide in matters of religion, which included such functions as determining the Jewish calendar for observance that would now be occurring in different time zones. And by setting up this new center of legal and religious decision making, he effectively transferred the role of the Temple to "wherever the leadership of Judaism had its seat."[28]

Ben Zakkai's first tasks were to negotiate favorable conditions with the ruling authority and to set up a durable form of institutional autonomy. Internal Jewish politics would henceforth require an independent legislative authority, while external politics—the equivalent of Jewish foreign affairs—called for securing the protection of Gentile rulers. The head of the academy, the Nasi, who fulfilled both tasks, became the equivalent of the head of a Jewish government in exile.

Though some interpreters of Judaism believe that at this point the spiritual essence of Judaism transcended its political trappings, as the soul may survive the collapse of the body,[29] in many respects, Jews were no less "political" in negotiating life in Yavneh than they had been when paying taxes to Rome from Jerusalem. Jewish centers in Babylon thrived for the next eight hundred years, and the Babylonian Talmud, which was codified simultaneously with the Palestinian Talmud, gradually became the more authoritative of the two compendia. The absence of a ruling ministry or national government was not acknowledged as a problem by those who took over the functions of a decentralized leadership.

This early example of Jewish adjustment to living abroad already demonstrates how mistaken was the later notion of the German sociologist Werner Sombart (1863–1941) that

Jews had remained throughout the centuries of exile "a desert and nomadic people."[30] Sombart, who coined the word *capitalism* and wrote a six-volume history of the subject, identified the Jews as essential to its development (Max Weber thought it was the Protestants). Sombart noticed that the European Jews had a keen ability to adjust to various cultures and circumstances, and from this he deduced that they were nomads or "Saharans," perennial wanderers who mastered trade and commerce in the process of migration. It was an ingenious theory, but one that drew wrong conclusions from accurate observations. The Jews *were* exceptionally adaptable, but they were nothing like nomads in their habits, social organization, or cultural inclinations. Nomadic peoples move cyclically or periodically, following the food supply of an agricultural economy or fulfilling the functions of tradesmen; their social, political, and cultural institutions are geared to the habits of frequent relocation. By contrast, Jews manifested the opposite penchant for sinking roots and establishing enduring institutions wherever they were allowed to do so. They negotiated their relationship with those in power, usually through the payment of taxes, trying to work out the most favorable conditions for permanent residence.

The Jewish polity in exile continued to model itself on self-rule in the Land of Israel, with this difference—that it handed over powers of protection to local rulers. In both Christian and Muslim theology and law, the Jews were tolerated aliens: the historian Yosef Yerushalmi has noted, "Given the irreducible difference and tension with the dominant religions, Jews were themselves inevitably conscious of the palpable differences that divided them from their non-Jewish neighbors. On this level one can safely say that Jews in *galut* [exile] were always aliens and felt themselves to be so."[31] But Yerushalmi insists that their estrangement paradoxically provided a core sense of identity, what he calls "the Judaization of exile." They gave Hebrew names to their places of residence and composed poems of appreciation for them when forced to leave.[32] They also invented their own founding myths: According to medieval legends, the city of Granada (*Granata al Yahud*, Granada of the Jews) was settled after the destruction of the First Temple in Jerusalem and received its name from the Hebrew *ger nad*—the wandering stranger who had settled there in ancient times.[33] Jews said that Poland (*poyln* in Yiddish or *polin* in Hebrew) got its name when the Jews arrived in the land and their leader said, " 'Here we rest for the night' [*po lin*] and this means that we shall rest here until we are all gathered into the land of Israel."[34] A city such as Vilna that acquired over several centuries the reputation of a place of great learning was called "the Jerusalem of Lithuania" and duly revered on that account. Physical remnants of the Jewish quarters of cities such as Rome, Prague, and Cairo attest to how long and resourcefully Jews sustained their communities in the midst of other nations. Yerushalmi calls this simultaneous fealty of Jews to the Land of Israel and to their places of quasi-permanent residence "being ideologically in exile and existentially at home."

The Diaspora experiment required creative accommodation to local political rule and socioeconomic opportunities. Look up the synonyms for *adaptation* and you discover Jewish communities at work: elastic, flexible, pliable, and supple, Jews tried to master the skills that would make them indispensable. These skills involved money lending, tax farming, minting, and banking; elsewhere it meant craftsmanship: They became shoemakers, tailors, carpenters, glaziers, all the trades that are turned into metaphors in the Yom Kippur prayer *ki hiney kahomer b'yad hayotser*, which likens material in the hands of the craftsman to the soul of the Jew before God.[35] The great historian Salo Baron describes how Jews tried to compensate for their political weakness with economic strength, even turning dispersion itself into an asset by developing international trade routes.

Sombart was so impressed with the energy of the Jews that he thought they were responsible for the modern economic development of Europe:

> It is indeed surprising that the parallelism has not before been observed between Jewish wanderings and settlement on the one hand, and the economic vicissitudes of the different peoples and states on the other. Israel passes over Europe like the sun: At its coming new life bursts forth: at its going all fall into decay.[36]

Once again, he mistook the part for the whole: it was the political patterns of host countries that determined optimal conditions for dynamic Jewish investment and commerce.

The increase of wealth in some societies as opposed to others was due not to the presence of the Jews alone but to the government policies that welcomed them and allowed them to create prosperity. Jews may have stimulated economic expansion and the spread of ideas, but only where they were invited or permitted to do so.

Features of the "Democratic" Jewish Polity

The story is told of a German intelligence officer serving in Warsaw during the First World War who was asked to investigate mysterious behavior in a certain Jewish courtyard. It had been reported that every evening Jewish coachmen would arrive individually and disappear into one of the buildings. The gathering had all the earmarks of a conspiracy against the occupying powers. When the officer went to investigate, he discovered the men seated at two long tables, bent over books, listening attentively to a teacher. The officer marveled to learn that these men had come to join in the study of the law after a day of labor. He was certain that he could find no such counterpart at the University of Berlin.[37]

No doubt Jews sometimes romanticize the importance of legal study in sustaining Diaspora life, yet it *was* the basis of their autonomous civilization from the academies at Yavneh to the courtyards of Poland. The democratization of education instilled what we might call a "constitutional culture" among not only the learned but all those who aspired to learning. Not everyone studied the Talmud at the same level of sophistication, but the simplified texts that these men were being taught derived from a common body of laws and conveyed a common ethical-moral instruction. Among the coachmen observed by the German officer were perhaps the father, uncle, and neighbors of the Warsaw woman with whom I began this book, whose idea of a decent human being emerged from the texts being studied around that table.

The voluntary nature of Jewish self-government contrasted sharply with the largely feudal, autocratic, despotic, or tyrannical political arrangements of the surrounding nations. Unlike those hierarchical societies that honored the divine rights of kings, Jews emphasized the reciprocal and communicable relationship between the King of Kings and man, authority and the people. Jewish self-government was as relatively open and transparent as the Bible's encounters between God and His people.[38] Abraham questioned God's moral yardstick on the destruction of Sodom and Gomorrah. King David at the height of his powers, when harshly reproached by Nathan, a man with no executive standing, accepted with the humility of a shepherd the punishment owing him as a sinner. Such expectations of justice informed Jewish self-governance through the ages. "The Jew complained about the leaders of the official community, their subservience to the [external] government and their unjust distribution of the tax burden; but he also taxed himself. He could hardly tell where discipline left off and his own sense of obligation began."[39]

Third-century rabbinic sources document instances of self-governance at all levels of Jewish society:

> The donkey drivers may declare: "We will provide another donkey to anyone whose donkey dies." If the death occurs as the result of [the owner's] negligence, they need not replace it; but if it is not the result of [such] negligence, they must replace it. If the owner states, "Give me the money and I will buy one for myself," they need not comply with his request, but they may purchase one and give it to him.
>
> The boatmen may declare, "We will provide another boat whenever anyone's boat is lost." If the loss is the result of [the owner's] negligence, they need not replace it; but if the loss is not the result of [such] negligence, they must replace it. If he [the owner] took it to a place where people do not ordinarily take their boats, they need not give him another boat.[40]

The insurance policies of the donkey drivers and boatmen were not open-ended: they provided those who had sustained losses with the means to continue working at the same occupation, not with loose cash for a vacation. Much as Jewish law governed its members, these associations assumed responsibility for only those members who intended to remain within the fold.

The representative body—kehillah or kahal—that typically administered Jewish communities from about the eleventh century had a board of elected and appointed members. It had the ruler's permission to levy and collect taxes for his government and to finance the community's educational, social, and religious needs. Benefits and abuses of this system obviously varied greatly from place to place, but even at the peak of kahal powers, enforcement did not depend on formal sanctions as much as "on the reputation of the rabbis issuing decrees, on public opinion and pressure, and on the shared values and interests (such as the strong urge to avoid creating pretexts for outside intervention)." The system rested mostly on voluntary consent. There was no binding final authority within the Jewish community. "In a very real sense, it was a government by consent of the governed."[41] Rabbis could intercede for their communities with God and the government, or rebuke the people for their transgressions. One Passover, having seen the working conditions in the communal matzo bakery, the Hasidic leader Levi Yitzhak of Berdichev told his followers, "The nations of the world accuse us of baking our matzo with Christian blood. That is a lie. We bake our matzo with Jewish blood."[42]

In applying the term *democratic* to Jewish self-government, Alan Dowty cites such democratic features as the strong incentive to give all groups a stake in the system, the essential unity that tolerated high levels of internal dissent, and the operational tradition of social justice and charity. Community leaders had to balance the need for order with relatively high degrees of personal freedom. This same decentralized political tradition prompted Israel's first elected leader, David Ben Gurion, to complain that he was the prime minister of a country of prime ministers. "Two Jews, three synagogues" is shorthand for such individualism when taken to extremes.

In spite of their dispersion, however, Jews experienced themselves as part of a unified people bound by the same national history and laws and attached to the same native land. Everywhere they observed the same calendar, trying to assemble, for example, according to the instructions in Leviticus, the four "species" of the Land of Israel—the *etrog* (citron), *lulav* (palm frond), myrtle bough (*hadas*), and willow branch (*aravah*)—in celebration of the autumn festival Succoth. Some Jews resented this collective identity: "Is there any other people in the world among whom the life of every individual, from the moment he comes into the world until his last breath, goes on and on according to a single pattern as it does among us? The way they are reared and educated, the words of their prayers, the tunes of their hymns and liturgical poems are all identical; even their food and drink are the same. . . . We are an ant hill, in which the individual has no existence apart from the community."[43] The grumbler lodging this complaint—the same Mendele the Book Peddler who cast Jewry in the image of the Wandering Mare—might have been surprised to know just how variously Jews had actually adjusted to local conditions. But he had a point: dispersed Jewish communities constituted a single variegated nation, and that Moroccan Jews ate rice during Passover from which Polish Jews abstained mattered less to national cohesion than the fact that every Jewish family on the same day of the Jewish calendar annually reenacted the exodus from Egypt.

Jews functioned as a nation despite their geographic fragmentation. The redemption of captives—singled out by the rabbis as a deed of exceptional merit—was so widely observed by Jews through the ages that slave traders and other traffickers in human cargo learned to exploit it.[44] Rabbinic authorities constituted the equivalent of an international court by trading opinions across countries and continents, with the locus of authority shifting according to the intellectual rise and decline of competing centers of learning. Basic uniformity in the liturgy allowed Jews to pray (in Hebrew and Aramaic) and participate in the Torah reading wherever they happened to travel. Because of the custom of preserving any texts that carry God's name— and a hypercorrectness that treated as sacred all texts transcribed in the Hebrew alphabet—Yiddish versions of medieval Germanic epic poems turned up in the depository (Genizah) of a Cairo synagogue, brought there by travelers who may have wanted to bed down with good entertainment in a foreign city.

Jewish self-government encouraged the development of a supremely competitive people, competitive because everywhere they had to prove their worth and could never take their existence for granted. Judaism's emphasis on universal education, personal accountability, and respect for the dignity of life encouraged individual ambition, while the traditions of mutual self-help forged the necessary discipline for survival in other peoples' lands. Habits of adaptation, acquired through displacement, stood the Jews in good stead, especially as the pace of change picked up in modern times, making the ability to adjust the most valuable skill of all.

The Politics of Language

Since the inauguration of the Nobel Prizes at the beginning of the twentieth century, Jews have received onetenth of its awards for literature: in German, Paul Heyse (1910), Nellie Sachs (1966), and Elias Canetti (1981); in French, Henri Bergson (1927); in Russian, Boris Pasternak (1958) and Joseph Brodsky (1987); in English, Saul Bellow (1976), Nadine Gordimer (1991), and Harold Pinter (2005); in Hungarian, Imre Kertesz (2002); in Hebrew, Shmuel Yosef Agnon (1966); and in Yiddish, Isaac Bashevis Singer (1978).[45] This exceptional roster of Jewish Nobel laureates in so many different tongues powerfully contradicts the essentialist connection between nationhood and national language that was postulated by the nineteenth-century German philosopher Johann Gottfried von Herder, and it points to contrasting German and Jewish notions of identity.

Beyond the disproportionate number of Jewish recipients, there are three unusual aspects of this statistic: the multiple languages in which Jews wrote; that there were winners in *two* Jewish languages; and that one of those languages was Hebrew, which no modern Jewish community had spoken before 1900. How and why did Jews develop a relation to language that was so different from that of their neighbors?

As regards Hebrew, we have seen that the prophet Ezra kept Jews connected to the Bible and to one another by featuring public reading of the scriptures as the core of public worship. Hebrew functioned as the spine of the Jewish nation and (with apologies for the awkward mix of metaphors) flowed as lifeblood through its veins. Strict requirements governed the exact transcription and pronunciation of the text of the Hebrew Bible, while the obligation of universal literacy, at least among Jewish males, made Hebrew accessible not just to the priests, as became true of Latin, but to everyone who ever attended elementary school and recited daily prayers. Biblical Hebrew was preserved in every jot and tittle, even as the language was put to other practical uses. In addition to its high-status functions of Torah reading and prayer, Hebrew was also employed in daily study and legislation and by the learned for personal correspondence. The rabbis who compiled the digest of the oral law, the Mishna, around 200 CE were already using and developing what came to be known as Mishnaic Hebrew, a language enriched by semantic and syntactic borrowings from Aramaic and other surrounding languages. Eventually, Hebrew served many worldly as well as religious functions, becoming a lingua franca for trade in the Muslim Middle Ages, when

Christians and Muslims did not know one another's tongues; during the high point of Jewish self-rule in Poland, when Jewish leaders conducted their own communal affairs through the Council of the Four Lands; and for Jewish messengers who required a secret code during the Italian Risorgimento. The blend of its sacred and secular functions through the centuries of dispersion made possible the eventual recovery of Hebrew as the national language of Israel.

As one demonstration of the function of Hebrew in Jewish life, we might consider the experience of the Reform movement in America, which until recently conducted its services almost exclusively in English, just as its parent Reform movement had done in German, in recognition of the inability of most of its members to read Hebrew. The move into English in the name of democratization had the opposite effect of limiting the conduct of the service to the rabbi and cantor. Whereas traditional Jewish prayer quorums—in which everyone knows the liturgy as well as the rabbis—are often led by ordinary members of the congregation, the obliteration of Hebrew from requirements for synagogue participation made Reform congregations functionally less "democratic" and at the mercy of a specialized elite that alone possessed access to the "original text." The current trend of Reform back to more Hebrew seeks to enfranchise congregants in Jewish communities of study and prayer. The centrality of the Bible in Jewish life makes the possession of Hebrew the key to individual autonomy.

Yet since most Jews probably stopped using Hebrew in everyday speech even before the end of the biblical period, the Bible had to be translated into the local languages that Jews actually spoke if they were to understand as well as to hear it.[46] The Aramaic translation of the Bible, the Targum, achieved near canonical status and is printed together with the original Hebrew in some editions of the Pentateuch. The Greek translation, the Septuagint, composed two centuries before the Common Era for Jewish settlers in Alexandria who had adopted Greek as their daily language, introduced the Bible to the outside world and enabled the spread of Christianity. The most frequently reprinted Jewish book of the eighteenth and nineteenth centuries, published in more than two hundred editions, was the Tsena Urena (Come forth and Behold; 1600), a Yiddish elaboration of the five books of Moses, with interpretive stories and homiletic teachings intended chiefly for women. English translations of the Bible, many of them intended for Jewish use, by now number in the hundreds.

Hence, the Jews' relation to language stands midway between Christians, for whom the Bible is the Bible irrespective of its language, and Muslims, for whom the divine word assumes an exclusively Arabic form.[47] Because Christians do not treat the Hebrew text differently from any translation, they considered the Latin Vulgate and English King James versions as sacrosanct as the original. The "Word of God" assumed for them any national identity into which it was transmitted; all nationalities can feel themselves to be authentically Christian. In the contrasting Muslim view, the Koran is only the Koran when it is in the original Arabic: it is the "Word of God" in the literal sense, and there are no translations, merely interlinear commentaries. A nexus of religious-national exclusivity reinforces the connection between Arabic and Islam and the division between Muslims from people of other nationalities.[48] For their part, Jews preserve the Hebrew text as the incorruptible source of their teachings while translating it into their languages of daily use. This reinforces national cohesion through interaction with surrounding cultures.

Hebrew was the central but never the exclusive Jewish language. From the Babylonian exile in 586 BCE onward, Jews did not speak a single common language. Because the fundamental unity of Judaism was more important than belonging to any particular geographic community, "language [was] not central in the traditional system of Jewishness: there was no concept of purism in the development of Jewish languages until the beginning of the twentieth century."[49] Reflecting on this pattern, the sociolinguist Joshua Fishman marvels at the almost complete lack of recorded laments in rabbinic literature over what must have been a wrenching transition from Hebrew to Aramaic, and from Aramaic to dozens of Diaspora Jewish languages: "Rabbinic literature pays almost no attention to intergenerational language discontinuity as either an individual or a communal problem."[50] Depending on local circumstances, Jews either mastered the languages of the surrounding populations or developed their own vernacular offshoots of the coterritorial language. Philologists and linguists study Jewish vernaculars such as Judeo-Persian, Judeo-Italian, Judeo-Arabic, Judeo-Greek, and so on for archaic features and terms that are lost in newer versions of the "host" languages.[51]

The two main Jewish vernaculars derive from the two main branches of Jewry: Yiddish from Ashkenazim; and Ladino, or Djudezmo, from Sephardim. The term *Ashkenaz* was applied in the Middle Ages to Germany, and later to central and eastern European Jews and their descendants; *Sepharad* became the term for Spain, and then for the lands where its Jews settled after the Inquisition and their expulsion from the Iberian Peninsula in the fifteenth century. Wherever the Spanish and Portuguese refugees settled in parts of North Africa, Greece, and Turkey, they spoke Djudezmo. The longer and farther they moved away from their place of departure, the more their language developed independently of its Spanish influence. In common with all Jewish vernaculars, it was written in Hebrew letters. In this way, the secondary languages of the Jews helped to preserve the alphabet and access to Hebrew.

Yiddish in its heyday was the most widespread of all languages ever spoken by Jews at a single point in history. It probably originated in the Rhineland about a millennium ago and grew more independent of its Middle High German base, just as Ladino did of Spanish when Jews migrated eastward.[52] To demonstrate the fused elements of Yiddish, which was sometimes suspected of being less than a "real" language, the linguist Max Weinreich constructed this model sentence: "Following the benediction after the meal, Grandfather bought a religious book: *Nokhn bentshn hot der zeyde gekoyft a seyfer.*" *Bentshn*, from the original Latin *benedicere*, came into Yiddish via an earlier southwestern European Jewish language spoken by Jews in the area of France; *nokhn*, *hot*, *der*, and *gekoyft* derive from the German, the main semantic source for Yiddish; *zeyde* is a Slavic component word for "grandfather," though no Slavic language has it in this form.[53] The word *seyfer* in the original Hebrew denotes a book of any kind, but Yiddish reserves this word for religious texts and uses the Germanic *bukh* for secular books. Consequently, despite the semantic predominance of German, the diverse roots and the transformative process of Yiddish would have made such a sentence incomprehensible to the average German speaker.[54]

A population explosion among Ashkenazic Jews in the nineteenth century created an unprecedented mass audience for Yiddish culture. Constrained at first by tsarist censorship, a boon in Yiddish publishing and performance soon produced a competitive theater, daily press, and elite and popular literature. By the time Isaac Bashevis Singer made his Yiddish debut as a writer in 1924 (alongside his older siblings Israel Joshua Singer and Esther Kreitman), Warsaw had become a hub of Yiddish literature and journalism.

Excluded from the Polish PEN Club, which restricted membership to writers in the Polish language, Yiddish writers appealed to the international organization for permission to form an independent Yiddish PEN Club within Poland, arguing that national language was not synonymous with national territory. Yiddish writers thus became the first to be granted membership in PEN as a national minority without a territorial state.[55]

The large numbers of Jews whose mother tongue was Yiddish (in some censuses as high as 95 percent) persuaded some modern ideologues that Yiddish could be the guarantor of national culture. They claimed on democratic or Marxist principles that a secular, modern Jewish national existence must be based on the language of Jewish majority or of the Jewish proletariat, and wherever ethnic minorities were allowed political representation in parliament, some championed Yiddish as the defining component of their ethnicity. Reveling in the political weakness of Yiddish— a language with no government or national institutions to protect it—the American Yiddish poet Moishe Leib Halpern proposed that if all declarations of war were henceforth issued in Yiddish, it would effectively guarantee peace in the world.[56]

Weinreich's model sentence anticipates why Yiddish culture could not sustain Jewish identity over time: the traditional Yiddish-speaking grandfather might go out to purchase a Yiddish book, but his pork-fed grandchild usually took up German or some other Western tongue. A language like Yiddish, generated by Jewish religious civilization to ensure its distinctiveness, was unlikely to flourish among secular Jews who were determined to take advantage of professional and social advancement in the broader society. Millions of Yiddish-speaking immigrants to the Americas quickly adopted the languages of their host country, in which they could take fullest advantage of their opportunities. Under Soviet Communism as well, most Jews shooed their children into Russian rather than Yiddish schools. Under conditions of freedom, only Jews who were as religiously observant as those who had created it in the first place clung to Yiddish. In fact, Yiddish still thrives today only where sectarian orthodox Jews try to fend off their secular environment.

The same political strategies of self-adaptation that once prompted Jews to adopt or to adapt coterritorial languages inspired some modern Jews to begin speaking Hebrew in everyday life. In an attempt to "normalize" their national existence, they felt they had to reestablish a normal national function for the only Jewish language that united Jews through time and space. In 1881, the first ideologue of modern Hebrew, Eliezer Ben Yehuda, explained to a friend in a Montmartre café his intention of settling in the Land of Israel. "That was the first time I spoke Hebrew at such length, and about such serious matters, and it was all done not for the sake of Hebrew conversation but for the sake of the subject matter."⁵⁷ The conversation lacked only certain specialized terminology, which he set about supplying. The rise of political Zionism at the turn of the twentieth century lent practical urgency to this spontaneous impulse, for how else but in Hebrew could Jews from Yemen and Ethiopia forge a common Jewish nation with Jews from Russia and Romania?

By the 1920s and 1930s, Yiddish was generating a world-class modern literature and culture, but the logic of Jewish politics demanded a common national language. Just as they had all along adjusted to local tongues, Jews in the Land of Israel now adjusted to a unifying Hebrew. Yiddish and other Diaspora languages yielded to Hebrew not simply because ideologues promoted it or because the state of Israel insisted on it, but on account of the political adaptation that required bringing Hebrew back into everyday use.

What a boon was Yiddish, with its stock of German, to Polish yeshiva boys who wanted to acquire the then dominant language of Europe! How exuberantly and efficiently Jews acquired, adapted, and abandoned languages according to whether they wanted more or less interaction with the surrounding nations! But Jews do not live in a political vacuum, and their linguistic adaptation looked very different from the contrasting perspective of those who conflated nationhood with national language. Jews may have assumed that their Gentile neighbors would appreciate their acquisition and cultivation of local language and cultures, yet the "multiculturalism" that Jews took for granted as a condition of their existence was often suspected of being a form of subversion by those in whose midst they lived.

Both Yiddish and German contain the sentence (here in its Yiddish version) *Vi es kristlt zikh, azoy yidlt zikh,* "As go the Christians, so go the Jews," a sociological observation that mocks the enthusiasm with which Jews habitually accommodate to the dominant culture. This enthusiasm for self-adaptation contrasted sharply with German attitudes toward *them.* German thinkers from Johann Gottlieb Fichte to Richard Wagner believed that German had special status as an *Ursprache,* or primal language, and that those who speak the same language "are joined to each other by a multitude of invisible bonds by nature herself, long before any human art begins." Germany could not absorb or mingle with people of different descent and language "without itself becoming confused, in the beginning at any rate, and violently disturbing the even progress of its culture."[58] Wagner fulminated against the Jews' "immature and incompetent knowledge of the German language," their too great haste in "appropriating what was too alien to them," and their consequent "falsification" of German purity.[59]

Germans coined the term *mauscheln,* "speaking like Moishe," to describe the unwelcome Yiddish-inflected Jewish jabber. "Elsewhere Yiddish sounded merely strange," remarks Steven Aschheim about the contact between Jews and other Europeans, "but in Germany it was precisely its familiarity that bred contempt."[60] Germans assumed that

Yiddish was a corrupted version of their perfect tongue. Jewish modernizers like Moses Mendelssohn, who absorbed German philosophy along with the language, were sometimes no less ruthless than their Christian counterparts in conflating the alleged corruption of language with the alleged corruption of its speakers.

Of course, Yiddish entailed no such degeneration. "Language is a dialect with an army and navy" was the retort of the linguist Max Weinreich to those who doubted the credentials of the Jewish vernacular.[61] In point of fact, the indifference of Jews to linguistic purity may have signified a "higher" rather than "lower" standard of morality: they refused to make a fetish of language or to value a cultural product higher than they did its creators. They were like Americans—promoting rather than preventing the absorption of "foreign" elements into their vital speech, just as they delighted in absorbing new ideas and readying themselves for new experiences. The generous attitude of Jews toward language exemplified their cultural fearlessness. "No other group betokened more strikingly the fact of change" is how the historian J. L. Talmon characterizes the role of Jews among the nations.[62] Germans mistook adaptability for negligence, creative energy for lack of rigor, and their own political might for evidence of moral superiority. By the end of the nineteenth century, the difference could not have been greater between the protectionist approach of many Germans to their national language and the eagerness of many Jews for cultural interpenetration. This contrast highlights the extreme divergence between Jewish nationalism and that of many others.

Jews were adaptive almost to a fault—or, rather, their acculturation was faulted by those who feared it. Jews considered it mutually beneficial to adjust to the nations among whom they settled. They did not foresee that some nations would distrust their adaptation. The Jews' unique relation to language, balancing national autonomy and political dependence, gave them spectacular advantages in cultural competition, but "landed" nations reserved the option of suppressing their competition by other means.

Jewish "Foreign Affairs"

In eighteenth-century Poland, most Jews lived in private towns, at the pleasure of the nobility who owned the land and the serfs. The story is told of a nobleman who decided to expel the Jews from his town, giving them a week to leave. The frantic townspeople ran to their rabbi, who promised to intervene. He screwed up his courage and went to see the duke, but all his pleas for clemency fell on deaf ears. Suddenly, the rabbi had an inspiration. Pointing to the dog that sat obediently at the nobleman's feet, he offered to teach the animal to speak. The duke was intrigued. "How long will it take?" The rabbi said he could do it within a year. "Very well," agreed the duke, "I will postpone the edict, but should you fail, the Jews will be expelled and you will be executed." The congregants were aghast when they heard these terms, but the rabbi reassured them. "A year is a long time. Before it is over, one of the two will croak—either the dog or the duke."

This joke gets across the high stakes of Diaspora politics, especially for Jewish leaders. The rabbinic concept governing Jewish relation to authority was *dina demalkhuta dina*, "the law of the land is the [Jewish] law."[63] Jews live by the sufferance of governments that have their own legal systems. What, then, is the relation between the two sets of authority? This concept would appear to consign determining power to the state, but since the rabbis are the ones promulgating this law, the Jews are technically under Jewish authority, deferring to the ruler on their own terms. In this way, the law of the state governing non-Jews is subsumed within the Jewish legal system and becomes binding also on Jews. Exceptions are made when government behavior or demands are considered illegitimate; for example, when they are directed at only one part of the population. The rule accepts the authority of the non-Jewish state while at the same time limiting its sphere of operation.[64]

The principle of *dina demalkhuta dina* worked itself out quite effectively in practice: Jewish politics was defined by the dependence of the Jews on Gentile sources of power. Tactically, Jews tried to achieve the best possible relationship with local authorities. Ideologically, Jews accepted that their pragmatic efforts to maintain the security and the stability of their communities were consistent with their efforts to follow the divine plan.[65] Jewish politics was shaped by the intersecting needs of accommodation to temporal authority and obedience to covenantal law. In trying to maintain this balance, Jewish life everywhere and always was determined by the best bargain Jews could strike with Gentile rulers.

Unlike the presumption of perfect justice that applied in the covenantal relationship between the Jews and God, Jews could not count on fairness from rulers no matter how scrupulously they obeyed their laws. Jews may have functioned autonomously in all other respects, but without political sovereignty they could not interact with other nations on equal terms. Instead of such normal formalities between nations as treaties and understandings (whether respected or violated), state visits, diplomatic exchanges, and so on, there developed between Jews and their hosts a *politics of complementarity* whereby Jews tried to win protection by proving their value. One side considered permanent a relationship that the other treated as work for hire. Unable to command the mutual recognition that territorial nations require from one another, Jews had to win toleration through exemplary behavior and proofs of service. The terms of these complementary arrangements varied from place to place, but Jewish activities always depended on the right to conduct them. The punch line of the joke, "either the dog will die, or the duke," tries to cover up the knowledge that, of the three, the Jew is the one whose survival is most in doubt.

Despite its dubious claim to historical accuracy, the biblical book of Esther—usually ascribed to the Persian period, before 330 BCE—serves as a kind of primer of Jewish foreign policy. The Persia of Esther's time is a cosmopolitan empire ruled by the despotic King Ahasuerus. Functioning without land, without central political authority, and without means of self-defense, the Jews seek protection directly from the king. At the start of the tale, they are faring well enough to incur the envy of the prime minister, Haman, who warns the king against them:

> "There is a certain people, scattered and dispersed among the other peoples in all the provinces of your realm, whose laws are different from those of any other people and who do not obey the king's laws; and it is not in Your Majesty's interest to tolerate them. If it please Your Majesty, let an edict be drawn for their destruction, and I will pay ten thousand talents of silver to the stewards for deposit in the royal treasury." Thereupon the king removed his signet ring and gave it to Haman son of Hammedatha the Agagite, the foe of the Jews. And the king said, "The money and the people are yours to do with as you see fit."[66]

The Jews of Shushan are prey to every schemer, but fortunately, in this case, their political skills compensate for their disadvantage. A certain Mordecai, self-appointed guardian of the Jews, had come to the king's favorable attention when he discovered and reported an assassination plot against His Majesty. Learning of Haman's plot, Mordecai persuades his relative Esther, whom Ahasuerus has made his queen, to help him thwart the conspirator. In the manner of assimilated Jews through the ages, Esther has not revealed her Jewish origins to the king. But when Mordecai appeals to her as a member of the community that is about to be annihilated, she agrees to try to stop the massacre and together they turn the tables on their enemies. Yoram Hazony reads the book of Esther as a study of "[how] the Jews, deprived of every sovereign institution of power, may nevertheless participate in, and in the last resort make use of, the authority of an alien government in ensuring their own vital interest, and in this case their lives."[67]

In this mythic account of their historical situation, the Jews are helped by the accident of good leadership. Had Mordecai not kept himself well informed of the goings-on in government circles, he could not have learned in time of the plot that Haman was hatching, and had Esther not been brave and resourceful, she could not have outmaneuvered the minister. Their high position in the royal court was not enough: they had also to demonstrate political initiative and take effective action. And because the fortunes of the Jews are subject to unforeseeable threats, not only from the king but *to* the king, Mordecai must protect the government that protects him. The unusual absence of God's name in the book of Esther underscores the Jews' ability, if they apply themselves, to score a political triumph without divine intervention.

Historical correspondences between this ancient story

and reality are often uncanny. Under the rule of Islam between about the tenth and fourteenth centuries, Muslim rulers elevated Jewish courtiers despite prohibitions in Islamic law against granting non-Muslims positions of authority. Acculturated to Arabic language and society, Jews rose in influence and accomplishment—even if not quite to Esther's rank of queen. During this so-called golden age of Spain, Jews developed a brilliant literary culture, flourishing international trade, and achievements in science, philosophy, and philology. The historian Yosef Kaplan points out that it was precisely the vulnerability and absolute dependency of Jewish courtiers on the ruler that made them (like Mordecai) so much more trustworthy than fellow Arabs, who might be scheming to take over the reins of power.[68]

Several centuries later, Jews of Poland believed that the story of Esther had come to life in the lovely central region of Kazimierz, where the beloved Jewish mistress of King Casimir the Great (1333–1370) is said to have influenced the king's favorable treatment of the Jews. King Casimir ratified the statute that his predecessor, Duke Boleslaw, had issued in 1264 granting Jews generous legal and political rights in the hope of attracting them to his region. He included specific points of protection from Christians, such as "It is absolutely forbidden to accuse the Jews of drinking human blood"; "If a Christian commits a depredation in a Jewish cemetery, he shall be severely punished by the confiscation of all his goods"; and "If anybody attacks a Jewish synagogue with stones, he shall be condemned to pay two pounds of pepper."[69] One of several reasons that Poland provided a relatively safe haven from the kind of persecution implicit in these injunctions was the decentralized nature of the Polish polity. Nobles who owned their towns competed for their Jews. Often lacking commercial or administrative experience, they leased their estates to the Jews in return for a fixed rent. Jews took over multiple tasks of production, trade, crafts, and supervision of agriculture, and flourished so visibly that a popular adage declared Poland heaven for the nobility, hell for the serfs, and paradise for the Jews.

The decentralized politics of the Polish realm allowed Polish Jewry to develop "the most elaborate and ramified institutional structures in European Jewish history: from artisan guilds and voluntary societies, communal governments, and regional assemblies to a national council or parliament called the Council of the Four Lands (*Va'ad arba aratsot*)."[70] The historian Gershon Hundert describes this council as a sort of bicameral parliament, composed of a lay assembly and board of rabbis, which enacted and put into force legislation on civic and criminal matters, and apportioned the taxes owing to the crown. Its biannual meetings at the fairs of Lublin and Jaroslaw became the occasion for all kinds of ancillary negotiations over everything from matchmaking to international commerce. Yet, here as elsewhere, the scope of Jewish self-government was subject to Gentile fiat. In 1764, the Polish government "disestablished" the Council of the Four Lands, and by the end of the century, Poland itself was disestablished by foreign invaders, each of whom claimed a portion of the country for itself. As if to signal the decline of Jewish political fortunes, some versions of the Polish "Esterke" story had the Jewish concubine killed during a pogrom following her protector's death.[71]

No matter how strong its leadership, Diaspora Jewry was everywhere subject to the whim of local authority. In Arab lands before the end of the tenth century, the Gaon, head of the yeshiva, was the undisputed Jewish religious, communal, and juridical authority, but as Shlomo Goitein puts it, the real power of the Gaon depended on those with the guns—on the Muslim government that had the military and police behind it.[72] The same held true for the Jewish elites of Christian Spain, who were protected as long as they were deemed indispensable to the interests of the crown; when the Inquisitors overcame the scruples of the rulers at the end of the fifteenth century, the king and queen ordered the wholesale expulsion of the Jews from Spain. The Jews of Poland were protected by royalty and the *szlachta*, the gentry, but only for as long as their presence was considered profitable. After the partitions of Poland, the Jews of Russia became wards of the tsar; later, under Communism, of Lenin and Stalin. Political complementarity meant that the greater the benefits Jews derived from those in power, the greater the rulers' power over them.

The No-Fail Target

I am hardly the first to discern that their political behavior made Jews a constant political quarry. The historian Gerson Cohen noted that "the safety of the Jews will always depend upon a society in which their interests are guaranteed and maintained," but that any breakdown of the social discipline within such a society exposes Jews to resentment and danger. He pays special attention to populist eruptions against the Jews that rulers and clergy are powerless to check. His earliest example of this pattern is the Jewish community of Elephantine in Upper Egypt, which was destroyed in 411 BCE:

> The Jews had been brought to Elephantine by the Persian government in order to secure the southern border of Egypt, but when there was no longer any need for their services and when, therefore, it no longer paid to defend them, they were abandoned. Similarly, the riots against the Jews in Alexandria in 37 CE occurred as a result of the Roman decision to abandon the best friends they had in Alexandria. . . . [The] Romans operated on the simple principles that politics is the art of the possible, and that the first thing the politician must do is to weigh where the present advantage lies.[73]

Cohen cites the Crusades of 1096, the Spanish riots of 1391, and the Ukrainian pogroms of 1648–49 to show how in each case the Jews were sacrificed by their erstwhile protectors to the violence of the mob. Jews had visible power and goods to tempt their assailants, but no means of defending that power and those goods once their political shield was withdrawn.

Jews were not the only group to hazard such conditions.[74] The sociologist Thomas Sowell explains how similar "middleman minorities" such as the overseas Chinese in Southeast Asia, the Armenians in the Ottoman Empire, and the Ibos in Nigeria, have all triggered violence on the most massive scale. "It is not just what these minorities have achieved, but how they have achieved it, that evokes suspicion and resentments"—the very functions of lending and charging interest, of bartering rather than producing necessities, trigger distrust. Envy and resentment are provoked not by wealth alone but by the intermediary role and social habits that set and keep these groups apart.[75] In the case of the Jews, however, this generic pattern was so much intensified through repetition as to become different in kind. To the Jews were also ascribed the religious betrayals of having denied the divinity of Jesus and the prophecy of Muhammad. Jews prominently served, more than other minorities, the "middleman" function in the realm of ideas and culture. Unlike other dispersed minorities that assimilated after three or four generations, the nucleus of unassimilable Jews stayed on or moved on elsewhere. In sum, the "ever-dying people" developed the world's most magnified image of the ubiquitous stranger—the "Wandering Jew."[76]

Examples could be drawn from almost every region to demonstrate how the attempt of Jews to sustain their autonomous way of life outside the Land of Israel inadvertently yet inevitably turned them into a no-fail target. At whatever point the ruler withdrew his protection, violence against the Jews was always profitable, either for him or for challengers he was trying to repel. Assaults on the Jews were without political consequence, as they lacked the power to retaliate, and rulers who had withdrawn their protection were disinclined to punish their attackers. Even when God occasionally did "punish" those who acted against the Jews—that is, when destroyers of the Jews subsequently went down to defeat—such posthumous victories had no deterrent effect on other enemies who failed to recognize God's hand in the matter.

The book of Esther anticipates this problem by settling scores in the here and now; the Jews turn the tables on their enemies on the very day of their scheduled massacre:

Throughout the provinces of King Ahasuerus, the Jews mustered in their cities to attack those who sought their hurt; and no one could withstand them, for the fear of them had fallen upon all the peoples. Indeed, all the officials of the provinces—the satraps, the governors, and the king's stewards—showed deference to the Jews, because the fear of Mordecai had fallen upon them. For Mordecai was now powerful in the royal palace, and his fame was spreading through all the provinces; the man Mordecai was growing ever more powerful. So the Jews struck at their enemies with the sword, slaying and destroying; they wreaked their will upon their enemies. (9:2–5)

To make this story politically persuasive, the biblical author knew he had to demonstrate Jewish power in unambiguous terms. Unless Jews inspired fear and encouraged rulers to protect them, another Haman would arise before this one's body was cold. Yet the reputation that Mordecai won in his time did not serve the Jews beyond his lifetime. Instead, the longer Jews remained in exile, the more they acquired the opposite reputation of being easy prey.

Occasional success through the intervention of a Mordecai or Esther notwithstanding, Jewish politics in the Diaspora was predicated on the assurance that God would someday honor the covenantal treaty and restore his people to Zion. The liturgy ascribes incredible power to God the Eternal of Hosts, Almighty, Ruler of the Universe, King of Kings: "The Eternal reigns, the Eternal has reigned, the Eternal shall reign for ever and ever. *Adonay melekh, adonay malakh, adonay yimlokh leolam va'ed.* The Eternal shall grant his people strength, the Eternal shall bless his people with peace." Since Jews consider themselves living proof of God's domination, their ultimate sovereignty is assured by their ultimate Guardian. In assuming the burden of God's Law,

Jews cast themselves as the human heroes of a divine struggle for redemption that depended on their ability to satisfy
the perfect and exacting Judge.

The Covenant of Sinai situated Jews politically not only
in relation to the powers that be, but in relation to the
Supreme Power who reigns eternal. "The day-to-day fate of
the people," the historian Yitzhak Baer wrote in 1936,

> is still completely comprehended—as it was in the
> days of the Bible—through a firm faith in the direct
> influence of God upon every historical event. This is
> no timid spinning out of old dreams, nor is it mere
> inertia under the burden of an incomprehensible
> destiny; rather, it is a system of religious concepts—
> complete in itself, if overloaded—of which every rep-
> resentative of the tradition can give a clear account.[77]

According to this two-tiered concept of potency, Jews were
not "powerless" at all. Indeed, it would have been immoral
to bring new generations of Jews into the world unless there
was a credible expectation of protection. Living in exile,
Jews tried to satisfy two kinds of rulers, only one of whom
was omnipotent and eternal. Such a long-range view of history subordinates or links immediate evidence of victory or
defeat to ultimate expectations, and encourages the capacity
for postponed political gratification.

In a Hebrew ballad by the poet Saul Tchernikhovsky
(1874–1943), three donkeys travel from Dan to Beersheba,

the proverbial length of the Land of Israel. The black donkey, carrying a great sword on its back, stops to kneel at a minaret. The brown, carrying a great cross on its back, pauses at a monastery. The white, bearing nothing, stops beside a ruin. The poem stresses that it carries *nothing*—but a golden rug that will someday bear the Messiah. The poem contrasts Muslims and Christians, who implanted mosques and churches on the land as symbols of their conquest, with Jews, who inherit the ruins and travel light, poised for the redemption they know will come.[78]

But non-Jews were entitled to draw more obvious conclusions from the Jewish "nothing." Christians, who anyway felt that theirs was a supercessionary faith, could and did interpret the Jews' dispersion as confirmation of Judaism's failure. Christian rulers did not recognize that Jews were subservient to God, but rather that they were subservient to *them*. Jewish political instability implied that God was punishing the Jews for denying Christ the Savior. Islam reached the same conclusion. Once Muhammad had defeated the Jews at the battle of Khyber, he, too, regarded them as political inferiors, a point of view that still governs Muslim political thought.[79] Jews (along with Christians) were *dhimmi*, followers of a tolerated religion that they could practice in private but under explicit conditions of political subservience. To both sets of rulers, Christians and Muslims, the Jews' lack of political sovereignty advertised their political weakness.

At Political Disadvantage

No matter how ably individual Jews abroad competed with others economically and culturally, the Jewish nation could not vie with other nations for political power. Jews could hardly aspire to govern a foreign polity when they could not even secure their own. For their part, Christians steadily expanded the power of the Church through coordination with the state. Legend has it that on the eve of the battle for control of the Western Roman Empire in 312, Emperor Constantine saw an imprint of a cross in the sky over the words, "With this sign you shall conquer." Formerly a pagan, he ordered the cross emblazoned on his soldiers' shields, and upon winning the battle over Rome's Milvian Bridge, he adopted the religion that had brought him victory. The conversion of Christianity into a state religion marked the turning point in the political rivalry between Christianity and Judaism.

As Christianity became the state religion in the Roman Empire in the late-fourth century, the Jews were suddenly conspicuous—"a large, well-organized, comparatively wealthy minority, well educated and highly religious, rejecting Christianity not out of ignorance but from obstinacy. They became, for Christianity, a 'problem,' to be solved."[80] Until that point, there were almost as many Jews as Christians in Europe, and Jews were as free to proselytize as they were to practice their religion (though no freer). From that point on, Christianity's power over Jews gave it advantages also in the war of ideas. Jews were forbidden to seek converts, and were made to live under conditions that advertised their inferiority to Gentiles. Thenceforth, Christianity could prosecute Jews with the power of the state, and the state could prosecute Jews in the name of religion. Even those Christian leaders, such as Augustine, who preached toleration meant only that Jews should be tolerated as witnesses to the triumph of the Church.

Their antithetical relation to political power exposed Jews and Christians to an opposite set of dangers. The more closely Christianity aligned itself with power and used that power to impose its rule, the more awkwardly it betrayed the teachings of the savior who had brought it into being. Contrarily, the less Jews felt empowered to advocate and practice their religion in an open marketplace of competing ideas, the more they were forced to make a virtue of weakness. Jews, whose religious teachings favored the robust responsibilities of a full sensual and political life over the ascetic tendencies of the Church, were increasingly forced into a defensive posture of protecting rather than promoting their way of life, and into martyrdom for their faith as the only alternative to conversion.

The worst effects of this political discrepancy between Jews and Christians were on display during the "disputations" of the thirteenth to the fifteenth centuries—public debates between representatives of the two religions that were, on the face of it, a civilized alternative to the earlier widespread slaughters of the Jews that had been triggered by the Crusades. The disputation was advertised as a superior kind of intellectual sporting contest, in which the relative merits of the two religions were to be determined on the plane of reason that distinguishes men from beasts. Replacement of gladiators by priests and rabbis, reliance on words instead of weapons, and recourse to religious debate in place of warfare seemed to play to the strength of the Jews by ensuring that they would not be disadvantaged by their military inferiority. The pretense of evenhandedness only heightened the unfairness.

The most famous of such contests, staged by King James I of Aragon in Barcelona on July 20–31, 1263, was the brainchild of Pablo (Paul) Christiani, a Jewish native of Montpellier who had converted to Catholicism, joined the Dominican Order, and engaged in missionary activities to Jews. Apparently frustrated in his attempt to influence his former coreligionists, Christiani persuaded the king to sponsor a public debate in which he, backed by prominent Dominicans and Franciscans, would demonstrate the truth of Christianity through recourse to the Jewish sources. Although the Jews placed their hopes in their spokesman—the foremost Talmudic scholar of his day, Rabbi Moses ben Nahman, or Nachmanides (known by his acronym Ramban)—and in the king's assurance that their champion could make his arguments without fear of punishment, they also knew that such a public "contest" could enrage the Christian mobs and their adversaries in the king's retinue.

Historians situate this debate and others like it in the context of the contemporary struggle taking place between Muslims and Christians, in which the latter eventually won control over the Iberian Peninsula. Jews had proven themselves very useful to both sets of rulers as administrators, advisors, physicians, and courtiers. In the process of acquiring the title "Conqueror," James I (1213–1276) had granted Jews favorable terms of colonization and various privileges and rights.[81] Once the Christian victories were assured, however, and Jewish influence began to wane, churchmen saw their chance to displace the Jewish "intruders" outright. The king may have felt no animus against the Jews, but there was always "the possibility of violence below the surface of urbanity."[82] Despite all assurances of safety that the king gave the rabbi in staging the debate, even he could not control its outcome.

That Christiani and the clergy should have sought this kind of academic confrontation suggests that they wanted to undermine the Jews in *Jewish* terms, that is, through force of argument rather than armed might. The Christian orders felt the need to prove their intellectual and not merely their political superiority, yet by relying on their power to ensure their victory, they forfeited any confidence they might have acquired through winning such an argument. They did not permit the Jewish disputant to do as they did in attacking the "lies" of the other religion, but forced him to prove that rabbinic sources did *not* bear witness to the Christian truth. The Christian disputants "not only engineered the confrontation but clearly stipulated an offensive role for the Christian protagonist and only a circumscribed defensive posture for the Jewish spokesman."[83]

Christiani flaunted his political advantage. In addition to the by then familiar contention that Isaiah's allusion to the "suffering servant" had foretold the coming of Christ, Christiani said the Jews' political history confirmed the failure of their religion. He cited Jacob's deathbed prophecy, Genesis 49:10: "The scepter shall not pass away from Judah, nor the ruler's staff from between his feet; so that tribute shall come to him, and the homage of peoples be his." The obvious failure of Jews to maintain their sovereignty, and their demonstrable political subservience to other nations, proved that Jews had forfeited their holy mission: "Since, therefore, it is certain that in Judah there is neither scepter nor leader, it is certain that the messiah [i.e., Jesus] who was to be sent has come."[84] There was menace as well as mockery in this argument. Supported in the debate by no less than the head of the Dominican Inquisition in Aragon, Raymund de Penaforte, Christiani was aware that the political dependency of the Jews was palpably manifest in their exposure to punishment by the Spanish court. As a convert protected by church and king, Christiani had good reason to claim that his adopted religion was more powerful than the one he had left behind.

Nachmanides parried with the argument that the scepter had not been removed from Judah but merely suspended, as it was in the time of the Babylonian captivity. (We recall that the Babylonian exile had become for the Jews proof of their resiliency rather than their demise.) He further distinguished between "Judah" and "Israel," noting that the "scepter" prophecy applies only to the tribe of Judah, not to the whole people of Israel as such.[85] According to his account of the disputation, he gave as good as he got. "[The] doctrine in which you believe, and which is the foundation of your faith, cannot be accepted by the reason, and nature affords no ground for it, nor have the prophets ever expressed it."[86] No Jew or anyone else of sound intelligence could tolerate the fantastical idea of a "virgin" birth. Moreover, history disproves the claims of Christianity far more than it does the claims of Judaism: Isaiah foretells that with the coming of the Messiah, nation shall not lift up sword against nation, neither shall they learn war any more (Isaiah 2:4), yet "[from] the time of Jesus until now, the whole world has been full of violence and plundering, and the Christians are greater spillers of blood than all the rest of the peoples."[87] Either in the debate itself or in his published account of it, Nachmanides appears to have gone on the offensive after all, questioning Christianity's claims to truth and citing its military victories as proof of its moral decline.

Despite the king's assurance of immunity, Nachmanides was charged with blasphemy and forced to leave Spain. The Christian account of the disputation indirectly justifies this act: "It was proven to [Nachmanides] that in Babylon [Jews] had the heads of the captivity with jurisdiction, but after the death of Christ they had neither leader nor prince nor the heads of captivity such as those attested by the Prophet Daniel, nor prophet nor any kind of rule, as is manifestly plain today."[88] According to this argument, the triumph of Christianity depended on the continuing political subservience of the Jews. Christians legitimated their right to subjugate the Jews as proof of the supercession they claimed. And contrarily, were the Jews ever to gain political independence, implying that the scepter *had* been returned to Judah, it would call Christianity into question. The historian Robert Chazan recognizes in the Barcelona disputation "an early harbinger of the crystallization of forces that would, over the ensuing century and a quarter, erode the material and spiritual strength of the flourishing Jewries of Spain," reaching their climax in the Inquisition and the final expulsion decree of 1492.[89]

Christians (this was also true of Muslims) used their political advantage to claim religious superiority over the Jews, but armed might could achieve only so much. Jews forced to convert under political pressure could hardly bring credit to a religion whose savior was martyred in defiance of political pressure. An inquisition that forced Jews to convert to Christianity could not trust the result of conversions gained on pain of death. The more aggressively Christians created converts, the less they could trust either the converts or their religion's spiritual claims to preeminence. Hence the political advantage that guaranteed the Church's supremacy also engendered its moral insecurity, since had it felt able to out-argue the Jews on their merits, it would not have had to rig the debate or persecute the debater. The self-doubt implicit in these disputations dictated a cycle of violence, since the allegations of superiority could be substantiated only through political force.[90]

These abuses of power gave Jews the intellectual-moral advantage over the Church. Neither crusaders nor jihadists, they were content to live among Christians, Muslims, or pagans. You could set your moral compass by the Jews: if violence and intolerance are considered evil, the protectors and defenders of Jews became the "due north" of the good. Whether or not individual Jews behaved any better than others, their patterns of political accommodation ensured that they would be the violated, not the violators. Jews who had taken up God's challenge to become "a kingdom of priests and a holy nation" found themselves involuntarily fulfilling that mission at the hands of Christians who betrayed their savior's calling.

Each new wave of anti-Jewishness, exceeding its predecessor in intensity, also exacted a steeper price for the privilege of remaining Jews. Theologically, how much Christian persecution could be accepted as just punishment from a just God? The experiential and moral rewards of the Jewish way of life may have been enough to nourish Jewish communities through the centuries, yet the punishing history of the Jews raised questions as painful as the conditions that prompted them.

Traitors, Informers, Casualties of Exile

The convert Pablo Christiani, who helped his adopted church subjugate his own group, recalls the historian Flavius Josephus. Jewish defectors were often invited not only to convert from one religion to another but to help prosecute their former co-religionists. Christiani used his familiarity with Jewish sources to discredit the community into which he had been born, knowing that they could, and probably would, suffer as a result. It bears noting that the kind of Jew that Gentiles were likeliest to get to know was the disloyal kind whose emergence they encouraged.

Foremost among the unattractive consequences of the Diaspora was the ubiquitous informer, or *moser*—the negative counterpart of the intercessor, or *shtadlan*, who speaks for the Jews to those in power. For every Mordecai and Esther who risked their lives to protect fellow Jews, there were schemers who turned betrayal or conversion to profit. The Jewish community was always hostage to its unhappiest members who stood to gain by serving the powers that be. Because of its limited ability to punish or control those who wished to defy its authority, the kehillah or kahal was rarely able to exercise the kind of punitive power that could have stanched the flow of defectors. Jewish self-government could not compete with Gentile authorities in offering its members political protection. As the Christian he became, Pablo Christiani manifested the corrupting potential of power, but as the Jew he was, the corrupting temptations of powerlessness. These two kinds of corruption are as opposite as the political traditions that elicit them.

The rabbis ruled against informers with exceptional severity. It was forbidden to inform on a fellow Jew to a Gentile, even about monetary matters, and even if the Jew was a sinful person. It was permitted to kill a person who was known with certainty to be setting out to inform on another—though only prior to his act of informing, not retroactively, not as punishment. It was permitted to kill without warning a person who regularly informed to the authorities. The harshness of these judgments are conspicuous in a culture that otherwise practically eliminated capital punishment.[91] Yet the community could not easily carry out such threats against informers who enjoyed authority's protection. Jewish humor concedes another sore point: One day a notorious informer is summoned before the town's rabbi and Jewish notables, who have finally got the goods on *him* and threaten to expose him to the authorities should he ever betray them again. The man stands there unfazed. "Why are you smiling?" asks the rabbi. The man replies, "Because I know that none of you is going to become an informer."[92]

Not every defector constituted a danger. A convert to Russian Orthodoxy, the noted archaeologist and professor of Oriental languages Daniel Chwolson (1819–1911) set the gold standard for wit when asked whether his decision to join the Church was made out of conviction or expediency. He replied, "I accepted baptism entirely out of conviction—the conviction that it is better to be a professor in the Academy in St. Petersburg than a *melamed* [elementary school teacher] in Eisheshok." Far from disparaging Judaism, he was reassuring his fellow Jews that he had merely chosen the practical advantages of the religion in power.

But if some renegades were harmless, others exploited the vulnerability of the Jews for gain. The most hurtful defectors were those whose sincerity prompted them to inform against those from whom they derived. Christiani anticipated thinkers such as Karl Marx who singled out the Jews for attack—in the latter case as the purest manifestation of the larger capitalist evil he was exposing. The same intellectual powers that sent Jews to the top of the Nobel Prize list also made Jewish anti-Jews more lethal than their Gentile counterparts. The Jews' political situation did not simply encourage acts of treason but ensured that their greatest "idealists" could do them the greatest harm.

Those who accuse Diaspora Jews of "dual loyalty" on the assumption that their clannishness would induce Jews to betray their countries of residence have not given enough thought to the political circumstances that govern the life of the Jews "in exile." It was politically illogical for Jews to betray the rulers whose protection they needed unless those rulers first betrayed *them*—and even then, how could Jews assume they would find any trustier alternatives? The advantages of power that rulers always enjoyed over their Jewish subjects made it far likelier that Jews would prove disloyal to their co-religionists than to those who could offer inducements for betrayal. Proving oneself to rulers was the precondition of exile; since Diaspora Jews in predemocratic societies accommodated to, rather than competed with, local sovereigns, they lacked the incentives for the kind of disloyalty of which they so often stood accused. Jewish communities did encourage internal unity, but rather than discourage political loyalty to the powers that be, their leaders usually required such loyalty as part of their demand for Jewish solidarity. Those modern Jewish revolutionaries who advocated the overthrow of governments were expressly defying Jewish leadership.[93]

Just as the Christian and Jewish sides each claimed victory in the Barcelona disputation, so, too, they drew opposite conclusions from their antithetical approaches to power. Despite the frequency with which Jews were attacked or expelled, Jews interpreted their survival as proof of their invincibility. Successive national disasters were absorbed into the day of mourning for the First and Second Temples. A modern anthologist of the literature of destruction, David G. Roskies, shows how each generation of Jews marked its own tragedies through the rituals and images of earlier catastrophes.[94] The Passover Haggadah reassures those who gather every year to reenact the Exodus from Egypt, "In every generation they stand up against us to destroy us, and the Holy One saves us from their hand," with the emphasis falling not on the catastrophe but on the ability to outlive it. The Yiddish poet H. Leivick (1888–1962) ends every stanza of a poem chronicling Jewish calamities with a testament to Jewish resilience:

> The world rings me round with its barbed hands
> And carries me to the fire, and carries me to the pyre;
> I burn and I burn and I am not consumed—
> *I pick myself up and stride onward.*[95] [emphasis added]

If Jews were the burning bush, then the auto-da-fé could be cited as proof that they were indestructible!

This pride in sheer survival demonstrates how the toleration of political weakness could cross the moral line into *veneration* of political weakness. Jews who endured exile as a temporary measure were in danger of mistaking it for a requirement of Jewish life or, worse, for a Jewish ideal. The original Jewish obligation to become for God "a kingdom of priests and a holy nation" called for the power to ensure human dignity. Jews may have lacked the military might to commit evil in ruling over others, but they were still obliged to uphold the good. What good could Jews do absent the power to act in history? The hostility of their antagonists sometimes trapped them in a political situation so dire that they could testify to God's presence only by how much indignity they could bear. This paradox was expressed with terrifying brilliance at the height of Hitler's war against the Jews by an anonymous Jew in the Warsaw Ghetto who said, "God forbid that the war should last as long as we are able to endure it."

PART TWO

Unanticipated Consequences of Emancipation

At length the day has come when the veil, by which we were kept in a state of humiliation, is rent; at length we recover those rights which have been taken from us more than eighteen centuries ago. How much are we at this moment indebted to the clemency of the God of our forefathers! We are now, thanks to the Supreme Being and to the sovereignty of the nation, not only Men and Citizens, but we are Frenchmen! What a happy change thou hast worked in us, merciful God![1]

In a flush of expectation, the Polish-born Jew Berr Isaac Berr greeted France's 1791 Decree of Emancipation—the first of its kind—and exhorted his fellow Jews to prove themselves worthy of the citizenship being granted them. God and the leaders of France are thanked for the new secular state that will accept him as a full-fledged Frenchman. Jews like Berr who had grown accustomed to the Diaspora welcomed the opportunity for French citizenship far more than the prospect of returning to the Land of Israel.

Legal emancipation ought to have alleviated the political handicaps of Jews in Europe by giving them an equal share in the obligations and rights that citizenship conferred. Jews would now serve in the military, pay no more than their equitable share of taxes, engage in any legal activities for which they considered themselves suited, train for the professions, and compete for whatever prizes the society had to offer. Though they might also produce their share of rogues and scoundrels, their punishments would now be only commensurate with their individual crimes. Wherever democracy made inroads, Jews would acquire the right to vote; wherever thrones toppled and hereditary privileges eroded, Jews could aspire to form part of government instead of being at its mercy.

Jews naturally differed in their assessment of what emancipation required of them. Berr Isaac Berr eagerly agreed to the separation of nationality from religion. Convinced by the pronouncement of the Count of Clermont-Tonnerre that "Jews should be denied everything as a nation, but granted everything as individuals," Berr wrote, "[It is] absolutely necessary . . . to divest ourselves entirely of that narrow spirit, of Corporation and Congregation, in all its civil and political matters not immediately connected with our spiritual laws."[2] His enthusiasm was not shared by the traditionally observant Jewish shopkeeper or his rabbi, whose Jewish way of life derived from an indissoluble fusion of religion and nationality, or by the kind of Jewish citizen, though perhaps no less eager than Berr to quit the ghetto, who was yet aware that as part of the process of secularization, Frenchmen, Germans, and other Europeans did not intend to dissolve *their* national identities. Why, then, should Jews be required to sacrifice theirs?

Jews' reactions to the promise of emancipation were as varied as the lands where they had settled. In Germany, where Luther had revolutionized the Christian religion, there arose a reform movement of Judaism that discarded such "repugnant" practices as circumcision and kashruth. In an attempt to denationalize the Jewish religion and make it more responsive to local citizenship, Reform synagogues replaced the use of Hebrew with German and no longer called for the restoration of Israel as the Jewish homeland. Championing the end result of such acculturation in central Europe, Stefan Zweig wrote approvingly that "nine-tenths of what the world celebrated as Viennese culture in the nineteenth century was promoted, nourished, or even created by Viennese Jewry."[3]

By contrast, the political struggles in Russia and Poland for freedom and independence touched off corresponding national impulses among their Jews. Several full-blown Jewish political movements emerged to offer competing visions of how a modern Jewish nation ought to function. Flourishing modern literatures in Yiddish and Hebrew furthered these tendencies even when their authors were not purposely driving any social or national agenda. Even among the

majority of eastern European Jews who maintained their traditional religious way of life, a newly defined "Orthodoxy"
formed its own political organizations and used newspapers
and other modern methods to strengthen its ranks.

The Damascus Affair

In February of 1840 an Italian monk and his servant disappeared from their cloister in Syria. Their whereabouts were
never discovered, and the "investigation" developed along
sinister lines. The rumor spread that Jews had murdered the
two men to use their blood for ritual purposes—a familiar
"blood libel" dating from the Middle Ages usually disseminated by the local administration or church. A Jew was
arrested, and under torture he identified as murderers the
most prominent Jews in the city. More of the same brutal
methods extracted confessions from those innocent community leaders in turn. Several of the men died in prison, one
converted to Christianity, there was rioting against Jews
of the city and region. The case threatened to remain one
more awful miscarriage of justice in a long history of Jewish
persecution.

But this was no longer the Middle Ages. European nations
competing for influence in the Middle East had consular officials in Damascus who tried to manipulate the case to their
advantage, spreading news of it to the continent, where it
soon involved representatives of all the major powers. Syria

was then governed despotically by the viceroy of Egypt, Muhammad 'Ali Pasha, who had won the territory from the sultan of Turkey. France supported Syria in the conflict; Turkey was backed by Austria and Great Britain. The Jews of Palestine and Turkey appealed for help to Jewish community leaders in Europe, who were caught off guard by the recurrence of so primitive a charge but then tried to rally to the defense of the victims. They soon discovered that the case was being treated according to narrow national self-interest: those governments opposed to Egyptian rule—particularly Austria—were far more inclined to intervene on behalf of the tortured Jews than the French, who wanted to reinforce their influence in Syria and Egypt.

Despite the personal involvement of the Rothschilds—James in France, Nathaniel in Britain, and Solomon in Austria—the Jewish intercessors could not initially win enough support to gain the release of the prisoners. Adolphe Cremieux, a Jewish member of the French Chamber of Deputies, and the philanthropist Sir Moses Montefiore of Britain traveled to Alexandria as ambassadors of the Jewish people to appeal directly to Muhammad 'Ali. They secured the prisoners' release only gradually, by the cumulative pressure of diplomatic interventions and of public protests as far away as America. Though it came far too late for most of the victims, the outcome allowed Montefiore to claim political victory. When the sultan assured him that Jews would enjoy the same privileges as all other peoples under his authority, Montefiore called the promise "the Magna Carta for the Jews in the Turkish dominions."[4] A more lasting outcome of this intervention was what the Jews created for themselves—a network of Jewish schools in Arab lands and, in 1860, the Alliance Israelite Universelle, an organization dedicated to the emancipation and education of Jews and the protection of those suffering persecution because they are Jews.

Jewish historians hailed the Damascus Affair as the first breach in the wall separating the "eastern" Sephardic Jews from their western brethren (Dubnow) and as a marker of Jewish political maturity (Graetz). Graetz felt the solidarity shown by Jews across the globe on this occasion had demonstrated "how wondrous the force which holds the members of the Jewish race in an indissoluble union; how strong the invisible bond which without their knowledge embraces them."[5] Dubnow noted that the political struggle over Syria and Turkey generated in some Jewish and Christian circles "Zionist" ideas of a Jewish center in Palestine while providing a political model of how such a Jewish national goal might be achieved.[6] Howard Sachar calls it the first time that Jewish emissaries had "evoked such an upsurge of spontaneous and collective Jewish action worldwide."[7] Graetz further claimed that the successful Jewish campaign of intervention demonstrated the advantages of Western civilization over the backward Middle East. As against the reactionary dictatorships with their barbaric methods of torture and extortion, the emergent liberal governments of Europe allowed Jews to lobby and to organize effectively on their own behalf.

But the affair also highlighted a new set of dangers inherent in the new Europe that were as yet unnoticed by those who assumed that theirs was an age of progress. Our contemporary Jonathan Frankel singles out the Damascus case for pointing up the paradoxical, unanticipated, and for a very long time unnoticed *deterioration* of the position of the Jews in France and in countries that were abandoning their hierarchical political structures. For one thing, it was the European consular corps, headed by the French consul in Damascus, that drove the prosecution relentlessly forward, and for another, the European press was reporting uncritically on the lurid charges.[8] European governments that had the diplomatic and political power to stop the case in its tracks failed to do so. Ultra-Catholics, who were opposed to Jewish emancipation, exploited the case to prove that Jews were not to be trusted with citizenship. Leading statesmen like the prime minister of France, Adolphe Thiers, temporized in coming to the Jews' defense, darkening the prospects for liberalism and human rights that they otherwise championed.

In fact, the new political situation in Europe proved more threatening to Jews than the old. "Stripped of the protection offered by state censorship, [Jews] could easily fall victim to a scandal-seeking press and to demagogic politicians outbidding each other for electoral advantage. During the

Damascus Affair, the Jews in France—and in the constitutional states of Germany—were deeply mortified to find themselves left almost alone to fight their own battles as best they could."[9] Blindsided by their apparent political progress and thrilled by the real augmentation of their civil liberties, Jews failed to appreciate that the replacement of a single autocratic ruler by an elected assembly had potentially reduced rather than increased their political influence. The same press that occasionally drew attention to their plight could also inflate demagogic accusations against them. The same politicians they tried to enlist in their defense could also sacrifice their interests to far larger competing constituencies. Their opponents were now freer to agitate against them with lurid propaganda disseminated through ever more sophisticated media. Seen from this angle, the Damascus Affair was a template for the anti-Semitic movement that arose thirty-five years later. As with Christianity, the real nature of liberal democracy depended not on its professed intentions but on how those ideals were put into practice.

The Emergence of Anti-Semitism

With the consolidation of the German Reich in 1871 and the adoption of a constitution extending the principle of equality to all citizens, Germany joined the European countries—France, Austria and Hungary, Holland,

and England—that had granted the Jews emancipation. At this juncture, Jews of western and central Europe could reasonably have concluded that they were becoming integrated into their host societies. For that very reason it came as a shock when "writers, politicians, and scholars again attacked Jews and found their onslaught so well received by the general public that a whole movement sprang up openly proclaiming its opposition to the Jews." The sociologist Jacob Katz notes that in at least one respect this new onslaught was more ominous than those of previous generations: accusations against Jews were formerly intended to keep them inside the ghetto, but leveled now, by fellow citizens, the charges meant to show that "Jews were unworthy of the legal and social position conferred upon them."[10]

The rise of anti-Semitism has been described so often we ought to have heard the last word on the subject, yet its ongoing vitality shows that no effective antidote has yet been discovered. When the carriers of a disease do not realize that they are its victims, they have no incentive to look for a cure, and (to continue with this admittedly imprecise metaphor) when the victims are not the main carriers of a disease, they can do nothing to stop the epidemic. Anti-Semites who organized their politics against the Jews saw no immediate disadvantage in it to themselves, and the Jews targeted by anti-Semitism were powerless to stop a movement that had them as its prey.

Liberal democracies are genuine to the extent that they encourage competition in goods, ideas, and human skills. So confident were the framers of emancipation of their political preeminence that they never considered the advantages Jews might have over them on a truly level playing field. Neither the German philosophers with their unacknowledged Christian prejudices, nor the radicals and revolutionaries who believed that political changes could level out human cultures, nor the liberals who feared the notion of a "chosen people," and perhaps least of all the Jews who assumed that *they* were the ones handicapped by history realized how advantageously the Jewish political tradition had prepared Jews for precisely the kind of open competition that they would be facing in an open society. But once the results began to show, elite reaction was very similar to that of the churchmen in Christian Spain.

> Why should I doubt it? A nation that is so keen on profit does not care whether it gets it by right or wrong means, by cunning or violence. And it seems made for commerce, or, in plain English, for swindling. Polite, pliable, enterprising, and discreet: these qualities would make the Jews admirable if they did not use them for our misfortune.[11]

The German baron who expresses these views in Gotthold Lessing's one-acter *The Jews* assumes that the rapid advancement of the Jewish parvenus tells against them, for how else but through unfair advantage could this politically disabled people have acquired so much prominence and visible wealth? This was the accusation that Haman once leveled against the upstart Mordecai, except that with the overthrow of kings, the Hamans were now jockeying for control of the citizenry. There was no better foil for the demagogue—who pretends to greater powers than he has—than Jews, whose image was so much greater than their political power. Lessing's play educates the fictional baron to recognize his mistake by making the anonymous rescuer to whom he confides his prejudice a Jew himself. But many a real-life politician met with no such correction when he slandered Jews to win over the crowd.

Political upheavals of the nineteenth century shook up populations that were far less accustomed than Jews were to tacking with the political winds. Institutions like the Church saw their authority declining. Industry uprooted rural populations. Established patterns of family and community succumbed to new demands for personal freedom. Technology spurred huge cultural transformations. Jews were familiar culprits at a time of accelerated change—a shared pretext for the nobleman who lost his property, the weaver who lost his customers to the machine, and the politician who needed an explanation for whatever was going wrong. The more perceptibly Jews benefited from modernity, the simpler it was to charge them with responsibility for its disturbances.

Spearhead of the movement that rallied Germans into a League of Anti-Semites was Wilhelm Marr's popular pamphlet *The Victory of Jewry over Germandom* (*Der Sieg des Judenthums über das Germanenthum*). Marr warned that, thanks to emancipation, Jews had already become the leading "super-power." "[In] Germany it is not Jewry that has merged into Germandom, but Germandom that has merged into Jewry. Merged to the point that the spokesmen for German patriotism, for acceptance of the new Reich, for our parliamentary, and yes, even our church battles—are Jews."[12] Marr, who had started out as a radical and remained a maverick, observed how successfully Jews were beginning to enter the mainstream of German politics, and how their erstwhile handicaps, such as decentralization and lack of military power, had been turned to contemporary advantage. "The Jews did not come to us as conquerors with the sword."[13] They did not have to: emancipation had allowed them to use their "cunning" to conquer the new country from within. "Since by virtue of our tribal organization we can never attain [the energy of initiative present in the Semitic race] and since an armistice in the history of civilization is impossible, there opens before us the prospect that someday the Jews will use the law and the state to attain a feudal domination over us. We Germans will become their slaves."[14]

In a joke with many lives, one Jew asks another why he is reading an anti-Semitic rag. The reader replies that whereas the Jewish press tells him only about Jewish disasters, the anti-Semitic press brings him the refreshing news that Jews control the world. There is no more flattering account than Marr's of the Jewish political experiment. His book and its later counterpart, *Protocols of the Elders of Zion*, say just what we have been saying: that Jews were exceptionally well prepared for liberal democracy. Unable to rely on coercive power, Jews had been forced to compete at a severe disadvantage. Like athletes that train with weights, Jews were more than ready for the competition once their handicaps were lifted. Marr simply reversed cause and effect, crediting the Jews with intentions of conquest for their successful attempts at accommodation. He ascribed to the Jews the quest for dominance that Christian rulers took for granted as the aim of politics but that Jews had jettisoned as part of their prolonged sojourn on other peoples' lands. The diabolical element in this accusation was to have charged the Jews with seizing the political power they were unwilling to wield. Marr's attack on the Jews would succeed precisely because they lacked the will to political power of which he accused them.[15]

A staunch enemy of religion, Marr distinguished his own brand of opposition to the Jews from the older forms of Jew hatred that were based on Christian mythology and medieval superstition. He coined the term "anti-Semitism" because he needed a concept that would impart "a new, nonreligious connotation to the term 'anti-Jewish.' "[16] The newer, more potent anti-Jewish politics was weighed down by no Christian inhibitions (even if those had been honored more often in the breach than in the observance) and no "fraternal" links with the "brothers of Jesus" to gnaw at the conscience.

Anti-Semitism put a Jewish face on all that threatened the security of the old order. To portray democracy, liberalism, and secularism as the work of the Jews "was a way of making these things suspect in the eyes of a growing but ill-educated electorate."[17] In his study of the links between liberalism and the rise of terrorism, Paul Berman identifies Lenin's Bolshevism as the first of the new anti-liberal movements to arise in Europe.[18] Actually, anti-Semitism antedated Lenin's movement by several decades. Rather than condemn outright such banner words as "liberty, equality, and fraternity," anti-Semitism accused them of being mere pretexts for Jewish domination. Other visible minorities, like the Gypsies, were not credible enough to be blamed for the problems of modern Europe. Christianity's obsession with the Jews had turned them into the most mythologized people in human history, and their exaggerated image was used to substantiate the charge that they were now exploiting liberal democracy for their own nefarious ends.

Karl Lueger was one of the first of many European politicians to win election, as mayor of Vienna in 1897, by holding Jews responsible for the shortfalls of the democratic polity that he intended to govern.[19] He offered Austrians security by promising to help them stop the encroachment of Jews, quieting anxieties with the slogan "The little man must be helped."[20] Opportunist over ideologue, he is credited with the motto "Who is a Jew, I decide," which he used to justify his occasional dependence on some of the people he demonized. Lueger ran against liberal democracy by promising to protect it from Jewish competition. No one ran against him by *supporting* the Jews, since even those who opposed anti-Semitism could hardly expect to win votes by extolling

Jewish virtues. Jewish attempts to organize against this campaign of defamation were offered by anti-Semites as proof of just how much power they wielded.

Protocols of the Elders of Zion was forged and disseminated as the Zionist movement was gaining momentum. The work purports to be the accidentally discovered proceedings of a cabal of Jewish conspirators. The secret minutes disclose how Jews plotted with the help of Freemasons "to overthrow all thrones and churches, remove all monarchs, destroy all states, and to erect on the ruins a Jewish world empire" that would be ruled by an autocrat of the House of David.[21] Another backhanded compliment to Jewish achievement, *Protocols*, like *The Victory of Jewry over Germandom*, assumes that a people *capable* of ruling the world must be planning to do so. The work interprets Jewish deference to power as a covert bid for power. "So-called liberalism" is the means through which Jews create anarchy, weaken authority, so that they can take up "the slackened reins of government."[22] Jewish authority pretends to be democratic, outwardly unsupported by force, the better to rule through secret sources of power that disseminate fear without appearing to do so.[23] Every humane value that Jews claimed as an attribute of their moral achievement is interpreted as a secret means to achieve world domination, and every aspect of Jewish accommodation is construed as a stratagem of conquest.

Jews believed that emancipation would give them a chance to contribute to their lands of citizenship. Anti-Semitism condemned the Jews for their virtues and charged them with exploiting the societies they hoped to join. Monarchists accused Jews of fomenting revolution and revolutionists accused Jews of being capitalists.[24] Nationalists found in the Jew the incarnation of who was *not* a Russian, *not* a Frenchman, *not* a German, Hungarian, or Pole. Socialism's substitution of class for nation encouraged the belief that since Jews had no country of their own, they should be the first to dispose of national ambitions. Not all parties and movements of Left and Right were anti-Jewish to the same degree, but each was anti-liberal to the degree that it was anti-Jewish. There were anti-liberal parties, like Mussolini's Fascists in Italy, that were not originally or innately anti-Semitic, *but there were no anti-Semitic parties that were not innately anti-liberal.*

Called "the longest hatred" for the way it served so many masters, defined as "the dislike of the unlike" for the way it turns on the alien "Other," anti-Semitism assumed in modern times a more precise political function that harnessed emotions like hatred and dislike to political tactics for political ends.[25] Its Christological origins and psychological features often obscure its political utility wherever public sentiment has to be boosted or swayed. Anti-Semitism was the perfect instrument of politicians who needed simple explanations for whatever was going wrong: the "Rothschilds" are stealing your money, the "Marxes and Engelses" are fomenting revolution; "the Jewish science," psychoanalysis, is corrupting our morals. The more proudly Jews contributed to society, the easier it was to demonstrate the threat they posed, and that alleged threat was reason enough to seize the powers and controls to check their advances. Opposition to Jewry was an amazingly effective tactic against liberalizing modern trends.

Jewish leadership showed itself ready, as in the Damascus case, to intervene on behalf of their co-religionists, but found no way of neutralizing the political assault. Kafka showed that the kind of reasoned argument one might introduce in a courtroom was beside the point when the verdict preceded the trial. If Jews tried to counter accusations of their wealth with statistical evidence that their masses were actually poor and needy, they inspired accusations of parasitism. Exposing anti-Semitism would have meant proving the corruption of anti-Semites, and who wanted to take on the most thuggish (and often persuasive) elements of the population? Disinclined to antagonize those whom they wanted to please, Jews preferred making themselves the subjects of humor: a self-accusatory people, they enjoyed joking about their flaws. My favorite of such quips is Shmaryahu Levin's "The Jews are a small people—but rotten." Habits of self-blame calculated to please the Lord were trotted out in climates of persecution.

Traditional Jews distrusted democracy for fear of losing their children to the new temptations of freedom, but those who embraced the new freedoms did not immediately see the dangers to them of a political system that rested on the "people's choice." Democracy allowed for, but was not synonymous with, a constitutional culture such as Jews took for granted in their own self-governance. The Jewish Diaspora entered its most dangerous phase just when it thought it had reached a safe plateau. Populations accustomed to tyranny remained susceptible to the appeal of politicians who offered what tyrants had delivered. Through their politics of complementarity Jews had tried to satisfy the requirements of rulers. Electoral politics now condemned them to satisfy leaders who could seek election at their expense. Underestimated by Jews, largely ignored by genuine liberals, and embraced by politicians of the Left and Right, anti-Semitism became the most effective ideology in Europe—the ideology of the twentieth century that came closest to fully achieving its goal.

PART THREE

Return to Zion

Isaac stood there on the soil of the Land of Israel he had yearned to see all the days of his life. Beneath his feet are the rocks of the Land of Israel and above his head blazes the sun of the Land of Israel and the houses of Jaffa rise up from the sea like regiments of wind, like clouds of splendor, and the sea recoils and comes back to the city, and does not swallow the city nor does the city drink up the sea. An hour or two ago, Isaac had been on the sea and now he is on dry land. An hour or two ago, he was drinking the air of other lands, and now he is drinking the air of the Land of Israel. No sooner had he collected his thoughts than the porters were standing around him and demanding money from him. He took out his purse and gave them. They demanded more. He gave them. They demanded more. Finally, they wanted *baksheesh*.[1]

Just as the Nobel-laureate-to-be Shmuel Yosef Agnon did in 1907, his fictional hero Isaac Kumer arrives to settle in the Land of Israel. Enthralled at having reached his destination, Isaac slips into the cadence of the Passover ceremony that re-creates the escape of the Israelites from slavery to liberation—before he was in the land of Egypt, now he is a free man. But "no sooner ha[s] he collected his thoughts" than the realities of the place begin to claim him in the form of Arab porters demanding their due—and more besides. Agnon enfolds the sublime in the prosaic to convey the mixed condition of coming home. Isaac's yearnings will henceforth have to take into account an Arab presence.

Jews had established permanent communities in the Diaspora when they could no longer defend their sovereignty in their own land. But by the end of the nineteenth century, their political experiment was in crisis on the continent where they had invested their greatest efforts. If, as Yiddish irony assures us, "God sends the remedy before the affliction," Jews had to find an alternative to their failing political strategy before it proved fatal. As their ancestors had once laid the groundwork for prolonged national life abroad, they now applied the many skills of adaptation acquired in the Diaspora to rebuilding a national home in Eretz Israel.

Over the centuries of dispersion many an impatient Jew had preceded Isaac Kumer to the Land of Israel.[2] Judah Halevi was born under Muslim rule in Toledo circa 1075, and, coming of age when the Crusaders marched on Jerusalem, he resented that others were laying siege to his sacred city.

My heart is in the East and I am at the edge of the West. Then how can I taste what I eat, how can I enjoy it? How can I fulfil my vows and pledges while Zion is in the domain of Edom, and I am in the bonds of Arabia? It would be easy for me to leave behind all the good things of Spain; it would be glorious to see the dust of the ruined Shrine.[3]

Halevi became a prominent physician and philosopher who adorned the golden age of Spanish Jewry. Well read in Arabic and Castilian, he chose to write poetry in Hebrew, and composed more than a thousand poems on secular and sacred themes, among which his "Songs of Zion" have been called the most passionate poems of the Holy Land since the Psalmists sang its praises. Around 1140, Halevi left his family to undertake the perilous voyage to Jerusalem. Whereas the biblical story of the Exodus recounted an escape of Jews from slavery to freedom, Halevi was quitting the glitter of high Spanish civilization for a distant city in ruins, exchanging privilege for poverty for the sake of returning to Zion. (The above translation of his verse is by the Hebrew poet Ted Carmi, who left the United States to settle in Israel.)

It was precisely this ironic twist in the Jewish story that appealed to Heinrich Heine seven centuries later, when he portrayed Judah Halevi "carried at the head of / Israel's sorrow-caravan / Through the wilderness of Exile."[4] Living in western Europe in the heyday of emancipation, Heine had himself baptized a Christian, an exchange he sardonically called his "entry ticket into European civilization." But he never stopped thinking of himself as a Jew. Toward the end of his life in a series called *Hebrew Melodies*, he compared Judah Halevi's "Songs of Zion" to the greatest love poetry of Europe:

> The one our rabbi [Judah Halevi] worshipped
> Was a sad, a wretched darling,
> Yea, the image of destruction—
> And her name—Jerusalem.
>
> Even in his early childhood
> She had been his only sweetheart:
> Even then his soul had quivered
> At the word Jerusalem.[5]

In Heine's version of the national love story, the Jewish poet-hero pays the ultimate price for his devotion to Zion. As Halevi sits at last among the ruins of his beloved city, he is stabbed through the heart by a passing Arab horseman. "Calmly flowed the rabbi's blood, / Calmly he intoned his song / To the last note, and his final / Death-sigh was Jerusalem!"

Heine threaded the sentiments of the Psalm 137 right through Hebrew poetry of Spain into the heart of nineteenth-century Europe, where they were picked up by many of the Hebrew and Yiddish poets he inspired. In the Jewish school that I attended in the 1940s, we sang Judah Halevi's poem in its Yiddish rendition by the Hebrew poet Chaim Nahman Bialik, who had written his own poems of longing for Eretz Israel before immigrating there in 1924.[6] A generation earlier, in the school my mother had attended in Vilna, she memorized Bialik's first published poem, "To the bird"—"*El hatsipor*"—which brings the poet greetings from the warmer East.

As nationalism began to claim the allegiance of citizens in emerging states of nineteenth-century Europe, Jews believed they, too, could resume their national life in their ancestral land. They witnessed Ireland and Poland mounting struggles for national independence against huge political odds. Moses Hess, Heine's contemporary, saw in the unification of Italy a model for the modern Jews' national reawakening:

> The nations of Europe have always regarded the existence of the Jews in their midst as an anomaly. We shall always remain strangers among the nations. They may even be moved by a sense of humanity and justice to emancipate us, but they will never *respect* us as long as we make *ubi bene ibi patria* our guiding principle, indeed almost a religion, and place it above our own great national memories.[7]

Hess perceived that in the new atmosphere of nationalism Jews could no longer honorably make their home wherever conditions were good—*ubi bene*—and he formulated the paradox that Jews could gain the respect of their fellow Europeans only by declaring their independence from Europe.

To the German-trained historian Ben-Zion Dinur, who immigrated to Palestine in 1921 and became Israel's third minister of education and culture thirty years later, the revolt against the exile seemed so powerful that it "forced the historical course of the nation back into its original channels": like a huge river into which flowed all the smaller streams and tributaries of the Jewish struggle down the ages, the revolt "incorporated into itself . . . all the various methods of resistance ever adopted by the Jews against their oppressors and persecutors, together with the stubborn persistence displayed by them in their hard struggle for survival."[8] As a rabbinical student, Dinur (né Dinaburg) had studied those portions of the Talmud that dealt with tilling and governing the Land of Israel in tandem with its more immediately relevant sections. Thus, even as he moved from Europe to Palestine, adopted Hebrew as his everyday language, and assumed a Hebraized family name to suit his new identity, he experienced his radical transformation as an organic outgrowth of his traditional upbringing.

Varieties of Liberal Zionism

The advent of anti-Semitism sped up a process of national consolidation that might otherwise have proceeded at a slower pace. "The more rational an idea, the less people are inclined to adopt it," lamented Moses Leib Lilienblum, a yeshiva student who became first a secular liberal, then a socialist, and finally, following the Russian pogroms of 1881–82, a passionate Zionist. Lilienblum admitted that when Wilhelm

Marr's "anachronistic" anti-Semitic diatribes surfaced in 1879 he had not taken them seriously, yet within three years he had been convinced of the need for an immediate exodus from Europe. The situation, he warned, was far more precarious than in the Middle Ages, when Jews could try to find temporary refuge in one place from their persecution in another. "The nations of Europe are just as adept in all branches of commerce as the Jews, so that they no longer need us. They are therefore able to apply pressure on us wherever and whenever they will— while we, where are we to flee?" Anticipating Hannah Arendt's analysis of the causes of anti-Semitism in her study of totalitarianism, Lilienblum pointed to the sudden superfluity of Jews in positions where they had once held sway.[9] Not a single European nation of western Europe was accepting any appreciable number of refugees from the Russian pogroms.[10] It was high time for his fellow Jews, who were "hated, hounded, beaten, murdered, and incinerated," to resettle in the Land of Israel, where they once enjoyed a national existence and where they might avert a future calamity[11]

Lilienblum's sense of urgency was confirmed when the "Dreyfus Affair" erupted in France—the country he had cited as the *exception* to the rampant anti-Semitism on the rest of the continent. A Jewish career officer attached to the General Staff, Captain Alfred Dreyfus was the ideal embodiment of emancipation as defined by Clermont-Tonnerre. Yet in 1894, when it was discovered that someone had been passing military secrets to the German embassy in Paris, suspicion fell on Dreyfus as a Jew. Convicted of treason by a secret military court-martial, he was stripped of his rank and sentenced to life imprisonment on the penal colony Devil's Island. The political Right turned the case into a judgment on the Jews and on the liberal policies that had encouraged their advancement. Édouard Drumont's mass-circulation newspaper *La Libre Parole* portrayed Dreyfus as the archetypal Jewish traitor. Monarchists identified his treachery as the consequence of Republicanism. Conservatives of every stripe, including artists and intellectuals, located in Dreyfus the proof that *their* France was being usurped by untrustworthy foreign inveiglers.

Many western Jews reacted to the Dreyfus case as Lilienblum had to the Russian pogroms: it was their 9/11, the attack that could not be ignored. Theodor Herzl, then a correspondent for the Viennese liberal daily *Neue Freie Presse*, was covering the Dreyfus trial as part of his beat. Herzl had stayed Jewish largely out of loyalty to his parents, and had once suggested voluntary baptism as a means of finally solving the Jewish question. With no reason at first to doubt the defendant's guilt, Herzl soon became convinced that Dreyfus was being framed, and then further persuaded by the anti-Jewish venom of the street mobs that the threat in France was not to Dreyfus alone. The atmosphere surrounding the case convinced Herzl that Jews desperately needed a land of their own. "I claim no new discoveries," he wrote. "I have discovered neither the Jewish situation as it has crystallized in history, nor the means to remedy it."[12] Indeed, had he been merely original, he could not have successfully organized the first Zionist Congress in 1897, or galvanized a movement that within a single year counted some eight hundred chapters across Europe representing 100,000 Jews.[13] The restoration of the Jewish state had assumed sudden urgency because "the world resound[ed] with clamor against the Jews."

Herzl's Zionism was anything but a retreat from his liberal aspirations. Though his manifesto, *The Jewish State*, resounded with national fervor—"We shall live at last as free men on our own soil, and in our own homes peacefully die"—he was quick to reassure his fellow Jews that if they later returned to Europe from their own country, they would be given the same kind of reception and treatment at the hands of civilized nations as the citizens of other foreign states.[14] Moreover, their national resurgence was also intended to profit others. "The world will be liberated by our freedom, enriched by our wealth, magnified by our greatness. And whatever we attempt there for our own benefit will redound mightily and beneficially to the good of all mankind."[15] He believed that in getting the Jews out of Europe, he would help to secure liberalism by removing one of its major irritants.[16]

The depth of Herzl's commitment to liberal ideals is touchingly on display in his utopian novel *Altneuland* (*Old-New Land*, 1902), which envisages the reconstituted Jewish Land of Israel as a more perfect miniature of Europe. The spokesman for the country explains, "We do not ask to what race or religion a man belongs. If he is a man, that is enough for us."[17] (The original German circumvents the gender barrier as well, using the neuter *Mensch* to designate the generic human being.[18]) In the Jewish state of Herzl's imagining, religion has been excluded from public affairs. People "may seek the eternal verities in a temple, a church or a mosque, in an art museum or at a philharmonic concert."[19] The place is governed by the representative council of "New Society"—an association of citizens that anyone may, but no one is obliged to, join. There are no soldiers or politicians: "Politics here is neither a business nor a profession, for either men or women. *We have kept ourselves unsullied by that plague*" (emphasis added).[20] Partisans of any kind are abjured, paid officials are not allowed to take part in public discussion, and only those who disdain the power they are expected to wield are elected. In the tradition of Moses and the Hebrew Prophets, only the reluctant leader wins the public trust. "Those who try to push themselves are gently ignored; while, on the other hand, we take great pains to discover real merit in the most obscure nooks."[21] Social arrangements in the country are so rational that they neutralize man's ego drives, including his will to power.

The most improbable member of Herzl's New Society is the Arab Reschid Bey, whom a skeptical European tries in vain to goad into admitting that he resents the Jewish new-comers. "Weren't the older inhabitants of Palestine ruined by the Jewish immigration? And didn't they have to leave the country? Don't you regard these Jews as intruders?" The pragmatic Bey scorns these provocations, explaining that

Jewish immigration benefited both prosperous Arabs such as himself and impoverished Arabs who gained means of livelihood and prosperity. "Nothing could have been more wretched than an Arab village at the end of the nineteenth century. The peasants' clay hovels were unfit for stables. The children lay naked and neglected in the streets. . . . Would you call a man a robber who takes nothing from you, but brings you something instead? The Jews have enriched us. Why should we be angry with them?"[22]

Never intended as a political blueprint, *Old-New Land* is revealing precisely because of how it replicates the adaptive policies of the Diaspora. Of the three staples of nationhood that Jews had lacked during their exile—land, central political authority, and means of self-defense—Herzl recovers only the first. The Jewish leaders of Herzl's imagined land want most of all to satisfy others—disillusioned Europeans who need a model of a truly liberal society, Arabs desperate for modern improvements, and assimilating Jews—probably the main intended audience for this German book—who must be coaxed into leaving Europe for their own good. Absence of an army and strong Jewish central government the author takes to be signs of human progress. All public spaces are non-denominational. No Jewish ritual or holiday is ever mentioned without the assurance that Gentiles are being included in its celebration. The only friction in this otherwise serene and pleasant land comes not from Arabs but from a certain Rabbi Geyer, "formerly an ultra-orthodox anti-Zionist, later a fervently religious nationalist, but always self-seeking, pompous, and repulsive."[23] Geyer wants a Jewish rather than a secular ecumenical polity, representing the kind of opposition Herzl faced within the Zionist movement (and disposed of much more handily in fiction than he could in real life).

Reproducing as it does liberalism's prejudice against many forms of Jewish distinctiveness and faith, Herzl's neutered version of a Jewish state was bound to offend Zionists with deeper religious convictions and Jewish cultural aspirations. Emerging from the Jewish heartland of eastern Europe, Ahad Ha'am (pen name of Asher Ginsberg, 1856–1927) dismissed *Old-New Land* as an act of pandering to the Gentile world. He was convinced that the material hardships of Jews could not be alleviated by the simple expediency of gathering them into the Jewish land, and that Jews had first to modernize wherever they were before attempting mass resettlement. He believed that Western Jews like Herzl would spoil the Jewish state in the very process of creating it. A Jewish state not rooted in Jewish culture "is apt to seduce us from our loyalty to spiritual greatness, and to beget in us a tendency to find the path of glory in attainment of material power and political domination, thus breaking the thread that unites us with the past, and undermining our historical basis."[24] In no rush to score political victories, he said he preferred "one solid excellent colony, whose quality attracted the people's love to the Land of Israel" to a rash of hastily established settlements.[25]

Ahad Ha'am's Hebrew essays were a healthy corrective to the sterile culture of Herzl's *Old-New Land*. Zionism needed an inclusive national language, a modern national culture, and purposeful national vision. But if Herzl lacked Jewish historical depth, Ahad Ha'am failed to grasp that Jews were running out of time. What strikes us today is less their cultural divergence than how little they actually broke with the past. Herzl imagines politics so divested of power that anyone who *wants* to be a leader is considered ineligible for the task. "If a demagogue were to try to incite my men," says Herzl's spokesman, "I should not need to have him thrown out—they'd simply laugh him out of court, so that he'd be glad to run away."[26] He replicates in the Land of Israel the political posture of the stateless European Jews whom he is trying to rescue. Ahad Ha'am invokes the spiritual legacy of the Prophets minus the potency of God's almighty hand. Jews had attributed to God the might they could not exert on their own behalf, but who did he think would protect "cultural Judaism" from the Jews' inevitable rivals?

Somewhat more sober than these Jewish proposals was the model of liberal Zionism provided by the British writer George Eliot in her 1876 novel *Daniel Deronda*, in which Gentile society is given at least some of the responsibility for recovering the Jewish homeland. The eponymous hero of this story is a citizen of a modern democracy, the adopted ward of a prominent Englishman and a member in good standing of British society, though he doesn't know quite how he fits into it. When he learns that he is a Jew, rather than try to become prime minister of England like Benjamin Disraeli, Deronda resolves to provide for Jews what the

British already possess. This requires of him a measure of renunciation, for in order to build a "national centre" for the Jews, he must leave the comforts of England behind.

> I am going to the East. . . . The idea that I am possessed with is that of restoring a political existence to my people, making them a nation again, giving them a national centre, such as the English have, though they too are scattered over the face of the globe. That is a task which presents itself to me as a duty: I am resolved to begin it, however feebly. I am resolved to devote my life to it. At the least, I may awaken a movement in other minds such as has been awakened in my own.[27]

George Eliot's Zionism derived—like Herzl's—from the realization that in a truly robust liberal democracy Jews would be regarded as political equals. In an act of renunciation parallel to Deronda's, her fellow Englishmen would have to let Jews realize *their own* national aspirations rather than insisting as the price of citizenship that Jews become indistinguishable from them. Although British liberalism was not xenophobic in the continental manner, Eliot found it guilty of wanting to smother non-Christians in its embrace. Some of the most misguided characters in her novel are also the gentlest, unable to understand why the Jews should not want to become Christians like themselves. As much to invigorate liberalism as to protect the Jews, she called for "separation with communication"—an ideal of genuine mutuality between mature nations yoked by strong bonds of respect and affection to one another and nations around the globe. This idea, though by no means dominant among British elites, made the case for a Jewish state part of the project of dismantling the British Empire.

George Eliot's novel features what the Jewish scenarios lack—a genuine villain, Henleigh Grandcourt. This menacing character, in perfect contrast to the Jewish hero, takes pleasure in the sadistic manipulation of his inferiors; his station and wealth allow him to "do evil" to his heart's content. As member of a society accustomed to exercising power, Eliot knew that the will to power, while perhaps not dominant in human affairs, could be exercised in democracies no less than in other political systems. In Grandcourt, she anticipated the black-booted and brown-shirted thugs who would soon be trampling the rights of citizens across Europe.[28]

From *Altneuland* to Tel Aviv

Actually, given the chance, most European Jews headed not for the Land of Israel but for America, in the time-tested manner of seeking out the society that offered the greatest freedom and opportunity. The pogroms of 1881 triggered the largest migrations in Jewish history: as compared with some 40,000 Jews who headed out for Palestine during the next twenty-five years, this non-ideological migration of more than one and a half million to America during the same period made it harder to convince Jews that the time had come to reconfigure a permanent home in the Middle East. Of the many movements vying for Jewish allegiance, none ever confronted Zionism with a greater challenge than the simpler option of moving to America, a land dubbed "Mother of Exiles" by the Jewish-American poet Emma Lazarus at the same time that she was herself being won over to the Zionist cause.[29]

There were also plenty of ideological alternatives to Zionism. About the same time that the British Jewish writer Israel Zangwill fashioned the American ideal of "the melting pot" in his popular play by that name, he wrote a story about a young Jew who tries to organize a unified Jewish self-defense in a Russian town he knows is targeted for a pogrom. Each and every faction that he approaches raises a different objection to uniting for action, prompting him to wonder whether Jews were "too sophisticated a people for so primitive and savage a function."[30] When the assault against the Jews finally comes, much more forcefully than he had anticipated, the young man shoots himself as the only certain means of depriving the enemy of his prey. Using this story as his outline, the historian Ezra Mendelsohn supplies a list of competing Jewish political factions around the turn of the twentieth century: "integrationism or assimilationism (of which there were two or three distinct types), Orthodoxy (also divided into two types, Hasidic and anti-Hasidic), several varieties of socialist Zionism, Zionist Zionism, cultural Zionism, Mizrachi (Orthodox Zionism), Sejmism, territorialism, socialist territorialism, and Bundism."[31] The same factionalism and traces of some of the same factions can be found in today's Israeli Knesset.

The Zionist impulse offered the clearest alternative to the young man's despair. Beginning about 1881, a voluntary migration of pioneering youth began building in Palestine the settlements and institutions of a Jewish country-in-the-making. Inspired by a visit to one of the new Jewish settlements in Palestine, the Galician-born Hebrew poet Naftali Hertz Imber wrote a lyric called "Our Hope" that was shortly after adopted by the Zionist movement as the Jewish national anthem, "Hatikvah," and slightly modified after 1948 to its present form:

kol od balevov pnima	As long as the heart
nefesh yehudi homiyah	of a Jew beats
u'lefatey mizrakh kadimah	and his eye is turned
ayin l'tsion tsofiyah	to the east,
od lo avda tikvateynu	our ancient hope is not lost,
hatikvah shnot alpayim	the hope of two thousand years:
lihyot am khofshi beartseynu	to be a free people in our land,
be'eretz tsion viyerusholim.	the land of Zion and Jerusalem.

This time, young Jews intended to reclaim their country and their political freedom through their own efforts. Pioneering settlers sang of draining the swamplands, irrigating the deserts, and restoring the biblical bounty of milk and honey. The term *aliyah*, ascent, signified the supreme value that Jews attached to this process: successive waves of immigration were numbered One through Five.[32]

Dvorah Dayan, the mother of one of Israel's military heroes (Moshe Dayan, the general with the eye patch), underwent a real-life transformation like Daniel Deronda's to become an immigrant of the Second Aliyah (circa 1902–14). The Russian-speaking Dayan realized one day that she was a stranger to the Russian poor among whom she had been working, and that her fellow Jews were strangers to her. Inspired by descriptions of Palestine that she found among her father's correspondence, she set out to join her people. "I know nothing of the land I am going to, and there is not a single person there I have ever met. I only know that there are men and women working for their people, and I belong to them." Once there, however, in order to become a member of an agricultural colony she had still to overcome the charge that she did not really fit in (she spoke neither Yiddish nor Hebrew). The task of baking bread for fifty people at last won her the satisfaction of belonging to a greater whole. "Close by, I hear the mill grinding out our grain. And the flour from the mill comes straight to me, and I bake the bread for all of us. Bread is surely needed."[33]

Herzl's novel, translated into Hebrew under the title *Tel Aviv* (Hill of Spring), lent its optimism and name to the first modern Jewish city that was founded in 1912 and soon filled with people from all over the world, as he had imagined. By the time Ahad Ha'am died in Palestine in 1927, a Hebrew university had been founded on Mount Scopus in Jerusalem, along with a network of Hebrew schools, daily Hebrew newspapers, theaters, and an academy of art. If idealism required placing the goals of the nation and humankind above individual ambition and assuming a life of great hardship for the sake of future generations, if it demanded faith in the values of justice and reason, courage to innovate, strength to labor, and sustained discipline to see the task through, then immigrants to the Land of Israel may have set the highest standard for idealism that any group—Jewish or otherwise—has ever approached. Mothers left behind the graves of their children, rabbis the prestige of their positions, adolescents their often comfortable European homes, to work as hired laborers in newly established settlements. In the struggling new economy, shopkeepers extended credit to needier neighbors, entrepreneurs created new products and jobs. Intellectuals undertook to drain the swamps, nonconformists submitted to communal regimen. Jews tried to subdue with the plow the land that Christians and Muslims had conquered with the sword. Through their collective efforts, the pioneers of Israel prepared a place of refuge for millions of Jews who were soon in desperate need of it. On their arrival after World War II, some refugees from the death camps were conscripted into the defense forces and sacrificed the lives they had saved with such exertion to protect a freedom that they had not yet begun to taste.

This panegyric is not intended to obscure the drudgery, pettiness, and misery in the lives of the settlers, recorded by them and in greater detail by descendants who often resented their parents' dedication to the Land. The impossibly high demands the pioneers made on themselves often yielded to disenchantment, sending a very high percentage of them back to Europe or on to America. Suicide and loneliness haunted the *yishuv*—the Jewish community of Palestine— despite and also because of its strong collective self-discipline. The conquest of the Land took a heavy toll on the founders of the nation. Dvorah Dayan, who so cheerfully mastered the art of baking and whose eldest son, Moshe, went on to become a national hero, collapsed when her youngest son was killed in Israel's War of Independence. After his death, "she was a broken woman. The light had gone out."[34] Isaac Kumer, who arrives so hopefully in Jaffa at the start of Agnon's novel, dies a very troubling death brought on by his own careless yet consequential deed. The builders and the chroniclers of Israel did not fail to register what was sacrificed and what inadvertently went awry in their creation of a new society. Successful accommodation required accountability.

Jews who resettled Palestine brought the Diaspora skills of self-adaptation to their highest perfection. Or, to put it otherwise, the politics of adaptation proved its ultimate genius in the building of Israel.

The Missing Component of Zionism

At the end of the nineteenth century, the Land of Israel was still part of the same Ottoman Empire that had witnessed and allowed the blood libel in Damascus in 1840. But the rise of modern nationalism was beginning to undermine the domination of European powers. Arab rulers who jockeyed for position in the Middle East enjoyed advantages of population over the Jews and a history of uninterrupted residence. Egypt, for example, had been Arab for 1,200 years since the Muslim invasion of the seventh century. While modern Turkey emerged from the Ottoman defeat much reduced in influence, the rest of the Arab world became the main beneficiary of the political reshuffle that resulted from the First World War. Britain responded to uprisings against its rule by declaring Egypt and Iraq independent in 1922, and in the same year established the Emirate of Transjordan (later Jordan) under the Hashemite Emir Abdullah. Syria and Lebanon took longer to free themselves from French control, but began positioning themselves during the First World War for the independence they achieved by the end of the Second. The seven Arabs states that formed the Arab League in 1945—Egypt, Iraq, Saudi Arabia, Yemen, Jordan, Syria, and Lebanon—were subsequently joined by Libya (1953), Sudan (1956), Tunisia and Morocco (1958), Kuwait

(1961), Algeria (1962), South Yemen (1967), Bahrain, Qatar, United Arab Emirates, and Oman (1971).[35]

Jews followed their traditional pattern of appealing to the good faith of stronger nations. Some Zionist leaders practiced diplomacy, Herzl negotiating with the Ottoman and European rulers, Chaim Weizmann with the British, Louis Brandeis with the Americans. The biggest such diplomatic gain—the Balfour Declaration of 1917—electrified the Jewish world. Issued by the world's then leading colonial power and endorsed by the League of Nations, it promised the "establishment in Palestine of a national home for the Jewish people." When he heard the news, my husband's grandfather, who owned a dry goods wholesale store in Montreal, Canada, declared a holiday for his employees and draped across the front window a huge blue and white flag that he had sewn in the design recently adopted by the Zionist movement. Britain seemed to have heeded George Eliot's counsel by assuming the role of Persia's Cyrus in restoring to the Jews their rightful land, and even those who did not pick up and move to Zion shared in the hopefulness of the moment.

The Zionist Organization concentrated on buying land and acquiring legal rights to the promised territory. The Jewish National Fund, established by the Fifth Zionist Congress in 1901, eventually owned about 20 percent of the land of Israel, and much more was purchased privately, for personal or institutional use. Raised on the biblical teachings that Jews had to be worthy of the land to which God had brought them, secular pioneers of Israel applied the expression *"kibush ha'aretz,"* "conquest of the Land," to the moral imperative of making the desert bloom. Socialists added the qualifier "Labor" to the term "Zionist," implying that the national impulse had to be tempered by an egalitarian ethos, and since Labor Zionists formed the earliest political leadership of the *yishuv*, many assumed that this "labor" qualifier defined the country itself. David Ben Gurion, leader of the centrist Labor movement, spoke for many in his belief that "[the] fate of the Jewish worker is linked to the fate of the Arab worker. We will rise together or sink together."[36] In their study of all that went into the creation of a new society in the Land of Israel, Ben Halpern and Jehuda Reinharz emphasize the "strange mixture of idealistic romanticism and pragmatic, if not opportunistic, realism pervading the history of Zionism in its every aspect."[37]

But notably absent from Jewish planning was the military force that every nation assumes it needs in order to regain, gain, or retain its land. Garibaldi's "one thousand," portrayed as a ragtag band of amateur warriors, nonetheless functioned as an army in the unification of Italy. The legendary national hero William Tell won his own and the nation's freedom through the power of his bow, and Switzerland maintains its neutrality at the heart of Europe with more soldiers per capita than any Western country. Insurgent and revolutionary groups of France and Russia seized power through terror, the preferred weapon of those who could not match the might of the entity they wished to overthrow. By contrast, Jewish memory lingered on the last military hero, Bar Kokhba, whose defeat by the Romans at the last mountain stronghold of Betar in 135 CE seemed to eliminate the option of Jewish armed might. Although scattered groups of Jewish youth, Zionists among them, had taken to organizing local self-defense against pogroms in Europe, such military action as Jews undertook in tandem with emancipation was performed mostly in the service of the armies of Europe.

The aberrant nature of Jewish political life became horribly manifest during World War I when an estimated half million Jews fought in the uniforms of the vying armies of Europe with no one to prevent the violence directed at *them*. The ethnographer S. An-sky reported on Jewish soldiers who went mad at the barbarism they witnessed.

> The human mind simply cannot grasp the horror of the events described in these and scores of other frantic letters [that An-sky was receiving from the front]. A region in which only yesterday a million Jews enjoyed human and civil rights was suddenly enclosed within a ring of fire, blood, and steel; they were cut off and at the mercy of frenzied and violent soldiers and Cossacks who attacked them like packs of wild animals. Many people believed that the entire Jewish population of Galicia was about to be destroyed.[38]

Stories circulated throughout the war about a Jewish soldier who hears the cry of "Shma Yisroel" ("Hear, O Israel!"—the

opening words of Judaism's pledge of allegiance to God)
from the enemy soldier whom he has just bayoneted: there
was simply no context for Jews to fight on their own behalf.
The Russian-Jewish writer Isaac Babel described in his diary
and the short stories based on his personal experience the
moral swamp he navigated as a uniformed Bolshevik in the
Polish-Russian War of 1920, having to pretend indifference
at the sight of massacred Jews and the suppression of the
Jewish way of life. Jews who had tried to live without enemies were now everyone's quarry, since no one was punished
for plundering or even murdering Jews.

Joseph Trumpeldor (1880–1920) was well placed to recognize the absurdity of the Jewish condition. A youthful
conscript to the Russian army, he lost an arm during the
Russo-Japanese War of 1904–5 but showed such qualities of
leadership that he became the first Jew under the tsar to be
granted officer's rank. After the war he studied law, then in
1912 gave up his commission and left Russia for Palestine to
join a cooperative settlement in the Galilee. When the First
World War broke out, the Turks expelled Trumpeldor from
Palestine along with many thousands of other Jews. He
found a chance to fight his way back when Vladimir "Ze'ev"
Jabotinsky conceived the idea of organizing among these
expelled Jews military units of the British army to help free
the Land of Israel from Turkish rule. The British War Ministry claimed that the Army Act did not permit the enlist-
ment of foreign nationals as fighting troops, but it allowed
them to enlist a volunteer transport group to convey sup-

plies and ammunition. Trumpeldor swallowed the indignity to him as a soldier and headed up the so-called Zion Mule Corps, which saw action on the Gallipoli Peninsula in the Dardanelles from May 1915 to the following January. By then a captain, Trumpeldor won from his commanding officer praise as the "bravest man [he] ever knew"—a reputation that followed him back to Palestine when he returned there in 1918 and was borne out two years later when he was killed successfully defending the northern Jewish settlement Tel Hai against Arab attackers.[39] He is best remembered for his dying words—*"Ein davar; tov lamut be'ad artzeinu"* ("Never mind, it's good to die for one's country"). Jabotinsky interpreted this to mean "Do not exaggerate; do not see danger where none exists; do not regard a man who does his duty as a hero—for history is long, the Jewish people everlasting, and truth is sacred, but everything else, trouble and care and pain and death, *ein davar.*"[40] Putting the emphasis on the end of his sentence rather than the overture, Trumpeldor may have been saying that he preferred to lay down his life for his own country rather than someone else's.

The first Jewish military leader since Bar Kokhba to die fighting for the Jewish nation, Captain Trumpeldor was an anomaly in the early years of Jewish settlement. In the *yishuv*, self-defense developed grudgingly and only in incremental stages. Hashomer, a small guild of watchmen, was founded in 1909 to guard Jewish settlements against thieves and marauders, but it did not prove up to the task of defense once local Arab nationalism assumed violent form. Not until Jabotinsky thought of organizing Jewish military units in the British army did Zionist leadership begin to consider the possibility of a Jewish armed force that would fight under its own insignia and flag. The "Lone Wolf" of Zionism (Ze'ev means wolf) and a consummate intellectual fluent in many European languages, Jabotinsky was, like Herzl, a successful journalist when he took up the challenge of providing Jewish self-defense, first in his native Russia, then for the Jewish state. Just as Herzl disclaimed any originality in calling for a Jewish state, so Jabotinsky denied originality in calling for a Jewish army: "As a matter of fact," he wrote, "this very normal idea would have occurred . . . to any normal person." But in Jewish colloquial parlance, the designation of "fully normal person" is sometimes rendered by the Yiddish expression *goyishe kop*, which makes it "so much the worse for us."[41] The Yiddish term *goyishe kop* invidiously compares a Gentile's intelligence to the shrewdness of a Jew. On the issue of Jewish power, Jabotinsky was saying that he wished Jews could become as simpleminded as Gentiles.

Jabotinsky's hard-won success in establishing a Jewish Legion during the First World War broke new political ground. By designating first one, then three battalions of Royal Fusiliers as Jewish regiments bearing the Jewish insignia of the seven-branched candelabrum, Britain committed Jews as a corporate body to one side of the conflict in which individual Jews were fighting under the flags of their countries of residence. The presence of "Jewish" regiments on one of the two sides provoked those who anyway suspected Jews of treason. What is more, with a Jewish legion fighting for the British, Zionism could no longer claim neutrality when it appealed to all nations alike for help in restoring a Jewish homeland. Yet the advantages of the venture far outweighed the risks: deported from Palestine by the Turks, Jewish leaders like David Ben Gurion and Yitzhak Ben Zvi (later to become Israel's second president) could now return to it in British uniform. To a people without a central government, the Jewish units of the British army demonstrated the value of a "Jewish foreign policy" as part of the international power struggle.

Jabotinsky expected the legion to become the nucleus of a Jewish army after Britain prevailed in Palestine. Conditions of the Mandate for Palestine obliged Britain to place the country "under such political, administrative and economic conditions as will secure the establishment of the Jewish national home . . . and the development of self-governing institutions"—which might logically have included a Jewish armed force to protect the centers of Jewish population.[42] But Britain categorically rejected the principle of Jewish self-protection, hastily disbanded the Jewish regiments, and imprisoned Jabotinsky and his associates for organizing self-defense in response to Arab attacks in 1920. For the next twenty years, Britain's Palestine policy followed the familiar pattern of rulers who appease aggressors at the expense of their Jewish populations. British acquiescence to Arab provocation forced Jewish self-defense in Palestine to form in defiance of the administrative power.

At its inaugural conference in December 1920, the Trade Union Movement (Histadrut) set up a national defense organization—Haganah—"to safeguard the national and social content of popular defense in this country," but no such defense was yet in place when Arabs rampaged against Orthodox Jews in 1929. That unprovoked slaughter of yeshiva students in Hebron and elsewhere marked a turning point in Jewish political consciousness in Palestine and beyond. In transplanting themselves from a more cultivated to an under-developed region of the world, Jews had hoped to find relief from the wholesale massacres to which they had been sub-ject. Yet here were pogroms just as before against the most peaceful segment of the population in a place where Jews had lived from time immemorial. It was from her burial place on the road to Efrat that Moses Hess—along with every other Jew who had ever studied in elementary school—expected Mother Rachel to be looking out for her returning children. The Hebron and Safed massacres finally roused the Histadrut to begin systematically training a Jewish armed force and to develop a military capacity that included the production of ammunition.

Arab insurgency grew inside Palestine through the 1930s in tandem with Hitlerism in Europe. Just when the Jews of Europe most needed a place of refuge, Britain bowed to Arab pressure to stop Jewish immigration to Palestine. In 1939 Britain issued a White Paper limiting Jewish immigration to

75,000 over the next five years, preventing the Jews of Palestine from saving their relatives just when Nazism was realizing its genocidal potential. Reluctantly, the *yishuv* realized that it would have to fight simultaneously on two fronts, as Ben Gurion put it, against the British as if there were no Germans and against the Germans as if there were no White Paper. This meant defying England to try to get as many Jews as possible out of Europe while urging the Jews of Palestine to join the British army.

Two competing approaches to the use of force in the *yishuv* then achieved in tandem what neither could have accomplished alone. Mainstream Zionist leadership adopted a policy of restraint, deferring to British oversight while organizing clandestinely against Arab terror. Jabotinsky insisted on more blatant use of counterforce against Arab insurgencies and quicker progress toward political independence. The Haganah promoted the discipline of an army, responsible to cautious political leadership; the Revisionists formed breakaway units of the Irgun Zsvai Leumi (National Military Organization) and followed the guerilla model of improvised raids to demoralize more powerful enemies. The two groups were adversaries: in one wretched period of 1945 known as "the hunting season," the Haganah helped the British track down members of the Jewish underground. Yet, in retrospect (and only in retrospect), the Haganah and the underground functioned as a good boxer's two fists. While the Haganah supplied the structure and discipline of an organized polity-in-the-making, Jewish guerillas matched threat with threat, and had they not done so, the British might have capitulated to Arab demands to hand them control of the country.

It was Britain that taught the Jews their harshest lessons in their attempt to reconstitute a politically grounded nation. Chaim Weizmann, long-term president of the World Zionist Organization and later first president of the state of Israel, encouraged Jews to regard Britain as their natural ally: he brought as evidence the liberal strain in British democracy represented by George Eliot and the Balfour Declaration and the emergence of Britain in the 1930s as the key defender of the democratic West. Despite the adversarial British White Paper, the *yishuv* followed Ben Gurion's urging to fight enthusiastically and with near unanimity for Britain during the war. Some four hundred new factories were built to supply Britain's Middle Eastern forces, eleven thousand Palestinian Jewish volunteers served in North Africa, and a Jewish brigade of volunteers was trained and sent for combat duty in Italy.[43] Yet at the end of the war, Britain felt no reciprocal loyalty to the Jews. Ernest Bevin, the same Labor leader who had once expressed sympathies for the Jewish cause in Palestine, turned hostile once he became foreign secretary of the postwar Labor government. He strictly enforced an embargo of Jews to Palestine, even turning back ships of Jewish refugees, while permitting unlimited Arab immigration into the area. Arthur Koestler, a European Jewish intellectual who made his permanent home in Britain, was provoked by the injustice of British actions to write a novel, *Thieves in the Night*, justifying the Palestinian Jewish underground's selective acts of terror against the British. All his bitterness about British policy went into the novel;[44] Ben Gurion's went into preparations for independence.

During a particularly disturbing period in the 1930s, when the British Royal Commission arrived to conduct one of its several inquiries into Arab violence against the *yishuv*, the future prime minister David Ben Gurion confided that he was less frightened by an external danger than by the naiveté with which Jews attempt to solve complicated questions. "We did not disappear from the face of the earth as other nations did, but we failed to remain independent in our homeland; we failed to save our state. This time our task is not to maintain a state but to build it; this constitutes a much more difficult political skill, and I do not see that we know it."[45] Many in the *yishuv* feared that fraternal strife—the haunting threat of those emblematic Talmudic adversaries Kamtsa and Bar Kamtsa—would prevent the emergence of the Third Jewish Commonwealth just as it had presumably brought down the Second, since the argument over force was only the sharpest of many divisions between religious and secular, Yiddishists and Hebraists, Left and Right, natives and immigrants, richer and poorer, ethnic communities from one another.

Yet fraternal strife destroys a country only when enemies are there to profit from it. Absent foreign invasions, the United States, for example, emerged physically intact and morally strengthened from its civil war of 1861–65. It was on the frightful battleground at Gettysburg that Abraham Lincoln proclaimed "a new birth of freedom" for the nation. An open society will always generate controversy, since liberal and conservative impulses always compete, even in one's own soul. The Talmudic tradition of argument and the decentralized nature of Jewish authority was bound to translate into factional rivalry within an independent Jewish state. Civil strife threatened the *yishuv* as it had the Second Commonwealth only because Jews came under foreign attack. "Kamtsa and Bar Kamtsa" becomes fatal when enemies can exploit the otherwise healthy tensions between political opponents.

Consider the fate of the *Altalena*. In anticipation of Britain's departure from Palestine in the spring of 1948, the Revisionists, headed by Menahem Begin, with help from his American supporters, had outfitted in France a ship of arms carrying guns, bullets, mortars, shells, and almost a thousand volunteers. Called *Altalena* after one of Jabotinsky's pen names, the ship "should have been a godsend":[46] everyone knew that the Arabs would try to take control of the country by force and that the Jews of Palestine were badly underequipped. Once Ben Gurion declared the state on May 14, negotiations had begun between him and Begin, his most serious rival for leadership, to include Revisionists in the provisional government. Begin was prepared in principle to merge the Irgun's military into the Israel Defense Forces that Ben Gurion had proclaimed as the "single army" of the new state. But the war the *yishuv* was already fighting in every part of the country impaired communication. The *Altalena* set sail from France under a veil of secrecy on June 9. Owing to a series of miscommunications and poor decisions, including the failure of his commanders in France to inform Begin of their plans, the Revisionist leadership in Palestine and the new government led by Ben Gurion were set on a collision course. The climate of distrust between the two sides fueled Ben Gurion's determination to come down hard against any threat of a separate armed force. Revisionists were afraid that they would be discriminated against in the new army and resolved to hold on to the arms that they had secured at such great risk. Whether or not they were explicitly ordered to do so, IDF soldiers fired on the ship as it was about to begin unloading on June 21, setting it ablaze and killing some of the fighters. Some two hundred Irgun men were taken prisoner along with their commanders. Yet though no other event in the history of the state reverberated with so many accusations and counteraccusations, the divisive potential of the affair was quashed by restraint on both sides. Menahem Begin, who had taken over as Revisionist leader, yielded military authority to the new prime minister, and within months, public pressure secured release of the imprisoned Revisionist leaders. The democratic nature of Israel was resolved, like the destiny of the United States by its civil war, at the height of sectarian conflict.

As the Jewish community of Palestine began to supply the military defense without which no country can expect to survive, leaders of both the Haganah and the Jewish underground assumed alike that this missing ingredient of Zionism would finally make Israel secure. Members of the Irgun argued that violence was "the new Esperanto" (referring to the international language that had been created by the Jew Ludwik Zamenhof),[47] and that only active retaliation would deter the Arabs from continuing their rampages. Both Jabotinsky and Ben Gurion eagerly looked forward to reciprocal relations with Arab and other nations. No one foresaw that Arab and Muslim governments, all of them anti-democratic autocracies, monarchies, and despotisms, would unite around anti-Zionism and try to satisfy their populations through the politics of blame.

The Tragedy of Anti-Zionism

Without indulging Herzl's kind of political fantasy, it is worth considering how the Middle East might have evolved had Arab rulers accepted the partition of Palestine (the remaining part of Palestine that Britain had not given to the Hashemites) into Jewish and Arab sectors as voted by the United Nations General Assembly on November 29, 1947. Some voluntary shifts of population would almost certainly have propelled Jews from Arab lands to Israel, and Arabs from the Jewish state into the Palestinian sector. Arab Palestine might have federated with Jordan, most of whose population is Palestinian, either under a single government or as adjoining states. Then, after modest territorial adjustments, regional priorities would have dictated new patterns of trade, commerce, and development. Those Jews and Arabs who wanted to remain in the other's land could have traveled back and forth between their communities and their transplanted relatives. The two sides had a lot to gain from each other in skills and natural assets.

But political reciprocity, whether in the form of trade, diplomacy, or cultural exchanges, was far from the calculations of Arab societies that had yet to undergo their own version of modernization. When Ben Gurion, taking a leaf from Herzl's *Altneuland*, assured the Palestinian Musa Alami in 1934 that Arabs had nothing to fear from the Zionists who were bringing a blessing to the Arabs of Palestine, Alami answered: "I prefer that the country remain impoverished and barren for another hundred years until we ourselves are able to develop it on our own."[48] Unlike the fictional Reschid Bey, most real-life Arab rulers saw the emerging Zionist enclave not as the neighbor or benefactor that Jews imagined themselves but as another version of the European civilization from whose oversight they were trying to emerge. The Arab Middle East had been obliged to defer to the Europeans who imposed their political rule through military superiority. No such consideration, however, was owed to Jews, whom other Europeans anyway held in open contempt. Given the fate of Jews under Hitler, their small numbers in Palestine, and the demonstrable reluctance of the British to defend them, Arab nationalists felt free to attack emerging Israel as proxy for the despised Europeans.

As early as the 1930s, Arab opposition to Israel could be

seen as resistance to the West. Leading the charge was Jerusalem-born Haj Amin el Husseini (1895–1974), who had studied Muslim law in Cairo, made the pilgrimage to Mecca, and served in both the Turkish army and the provisional British military government before joining an Arab nationalist group that called for the incorporation of Palestine into greater Syria. Husseini pioneered anti-Jewish terror in an attack at the Western Wall in Jerusalem in 1920. Sentenced by a British military court, he was pardoned a year later by the British high commissioner in Palestine, Sir Herbert Samuel, a Jew who may have been eager to prove his "impartiality" in the local conflict. In 1921 Samuel tried to co-opt Husseini by appointing him Grand Mufti of Jerusalem. The Mufti revved up attacks on Jews and used his position to terrorize Arab rivals—a pattern later repeated by the head of the Palestinian Liberation Organization, Yasser Arafat (who boasted of being of the same Husseini clan). In 1929, Husseini organized full-scale pogroms against Jewish religious students in Safed and Hebron, and in 1936–37 he engineered the "great revolt" against British rule. Appointed leader of the first Supreme Muslim Council, he injected "a religious character into the struggle against Zionism" and an extremist character into the practice of Islam.[49] Even after he fled deportation in 1937, he continued to direct anti-Jewish and anti-British actions from outside the country. During World War II, he zigzagged between Rome and Berlin, offering to lead "the Arab nation" in the war against their common enemy, Britain, helping to found Muslim SS divisions and personally intervening to prevent the rescue of Jewish war orphans.[50] This was one of the many doors through which Nazi anti-Semitism penetrated Arab societies.

In an effort to extend Soviet influence in the Middle East, Joseph Stalin hailed Amin el Husseini's anti-Jewish attacks as the spearhead of an Arab uprising against British and Zionist imperialism. Stalin's support of anti-Jewish violence in Palestine served a number of domestic as well as international aims, including the hope of placating Muslims who formed a fifth of the Soviet population. Communism opposed Jewish nationalism as a reactionary deviation from class conflict, and expected Jews, who did not yet have a land of their own, to be the first to divest themselves of their national particularity. To counteract the growing enthusiasm for Zionism that was nonetheless spreading among Russian Jews, Stalin set up an "autonomous Jewish territory" in the easternmost part of Russia as an alternative to Palestine while simultaneously outlawing the use of Hebrew and other manifestations of support for a Jewish homeland. He now added to earlier accusations of reactionary Jewish nationalism the charge of Jewish imperialism in Palestine, laying the groundwork for the transition from anti-Semitism to anti-Zionism. Communists around the world took up this line. At the Comintern (Communist International) Congress of 1935, the Arab delegate from Palestine characterized Zionism as a bourgeois movement, a colonial outpost supported by English imperialism: "Zionist capital not only directly oppresses the Arab working masses, but ruthlessly annihilates the petite bourgeoisie and in a huge way pushes out the middle and even the highest strata of the Arab commercial and industrial bourgeoisie."[51]

Arab opposition to the Jews drew support from all the anti-democratic factions. Most Arab rulers took the side of the Axis during the Second World War, either by joining the war, like Iraq, or by withholding support for the Allies and sheltering Nazis in its aftermath. While Arabs on the Right sided with the Nazis, Arabs on the Left presented themselves as victims of Jewish imperialist forces. The Arab Right threatened to crush those whom the Arab Left claimed to be crushed by. This apparent contradiction appealed to both traditional and radical Arab constituencies. It was always plausible to accuse Jews of causing Arab misery since, compared to Jews, the Arab masses *were* disadvantaged, held back by their political leadership.

In 1945, an exhausted Western Alliance set up the United Nations, "determined to save succeeding generations from the scourge of war."[52] One of its first challenges was to redress the crime done to the Jews by ceding to them the land they had been promised by Britain and the League of Nations. But as Jews tried to garner support for the partition of Palestine, Arab leaders organized the League of Arab States to block emergence of the promised Jewish homeland. Rejecting any compromise out of hand, they claimed that a preexisting Arab state already occupied the entire territory of British Mandate Palestine: "Her international existence and independence in the legal sense cannot therefore be questioned, any more than could the independence of the other Arab countries."[53] Since no such state actually existed, the League proposed to take charge of its destiny until an "independent" Palestine could effectively govern itself. Members of the League used the pretext of protecting Arab Palestine to justify their opposition to partition of the territory, thereby equally denying Jews and Palestinian Arabs the possibility of political autonomy.

The prospect for territorial compromise was not entirely absent in the Arab world. King Abdullah I of Jordan (1882– 1951), whose loyalties were with the British, harbored his own dreams of a far-reaching Hashemite kingdom, but he was ready to discuss a peace treaty with Israel as part of his plan for a regional settlement. His assassination by loyalists of the Husseini clan in 1951 at the entrance of the Al Aqsa Mosque in Jerusalem foreclosed such a possibility. Although the secret meeting between Abdullah and Ben Gurion's representative—the future prime minister Golda Meir disguised as a male Arab—became part of Israeli lore, and though Abdullah's grandson and successor, King Hussein, was a relatively Western-tending ruler, Jordan remained a solid member of the Arab League and joined in the wars against Israel in 1967. The fate of King Abdullah as an Arab "moderate" proved an augury for the fate of regional peace.

The Innovations of Anti-Zionism

In 1947, during the interval between the destruction of European Jewry and the creation of Israel, the American-Jewish cartoonist Al Capp (Alfred Gerald Caplin, 1909–1979) invented a jinxed character, Joe Btfsplk, who always appears with a black cloud over his head. The political hostility aimed at the Jews is like that cloud, following them wherever they go, independently of their actions, making them unpopular even among people who would otherwise rise to their defense. The cloud darkens what might otherwise be a radiant story of Jewish acccomplishment. As the Jews concentrated in a new center, new coalitions formed against them. Once damned for their lack of power, Jews would now be accused of becoming too strong.

When protests erupted in 2005 against the Iranian president Mahmoud Ahmadinejad's call for Israel to be "wiped off the map," the editor of an Iranian daily protested, "Our respected president has not said anything new or unprecedented about Israel to justify such a huge political tumult."[54] He was right: Arab leaders had been calling for the elimination of Israel since its creation. Herzl and his fellow Zionists had thought they identified in Jewish statelessness the critical variable of European anti-Semitism, but their commonsensical deduction did not get to the heart of the matter. Unable to see themselves through the eyes of their enemies, they could not fathom that their utility as a political target rather than their actions defined their role in the politics of their opponents. The animus against them was not directed to any *correctable* attribute or rectifiable lapses. What was true in late-nineteenth-century Europe became even truer in the Middle East: Jews created in Israel the same potential for anti-Jewish politics as had been directed until then against the stateless Jews. Anti-Zionism (the organization of politics in opposition to Israel) went beyond anti-Semitism (the organization of politics in opposition to the Jews), just as anti-Semitism had superceded the Judeophobia of the Church (the organization of politics against the Jewish religion).

Anti-Semitism had emerged in Europe on a country-by-country basis, with every nation supplying its own politicians and parties: Nazi Germany took the lead in anti-Jewish propaganda, but without ever organizing a Pan-European movement around that issue. By contrast, opposition to Israel became the glue of Pan-Arabism and, later, Islamism. Although in theory there might have been many positive reasons for Arab-speaking countries to cooperate around economic, political, and cultural goals, the Arab League actually formed in 1945 around the goal of preventing the emergence of the Jewish state. Common opposition to Israel remains to the present day the strongest unifying political element among Arab and Muslim countries that otherwise compete with one another. The first time modern Arab armies joined together in battle was to invade Israel on the day of its founding.

The boycott of Jewish stores and businesses had been a frequent but sporadic feature of nationalist politics in the 1930s. Poland's *Swoj do swego* and Quebec's *Achetez chez nous* were local and temporary movements to steer consumers away from Jewish to "native-run" businesses. The Arab League organized its boycott of "Jewish products and manufactured goods" much more systematically and on an international basis, bringing the full weight of its diplomatic and purchasing power to bear on those who did business with Jews. The Arab Bureau for the Boycott of Israel used the resources and influence of Arab and Muslim countries to isolate Israel, and enjoyed the power it thereby derived from controlling international traffic. The boycott prohibits direct trade between Israel and the Arab nations, trade with companies that do business with Israel, and trade with firms that trade with other companies that do business with Israel— many thousands of companies and persons since 1951.[55] Although the embargo weakened somewhat under American pressure, its sanctions were upheld at the seventy-second meeting in Syria in 2004.[56]

Whereas Hitler had to function as his own impresario in organizing mass rallies, parades, and "spontaneous" demonstrations, Arab rulers use weapons of mass communication. A televised version of *Protocols of the Elders of Zion* recently broadcast throughout the Arab world brought evil caricatures of Jews into the homes of millions who have never seen a Jew before. The potential for such propaganda was greatly boosted by early UN recognition of the Arab League as the official organization for education, science, and culture in the Arab region, allowing the spread of anti-Jewish and anti-Israel defamation as a sanctioned element of Arab culture.

Although European anti-Semites blamed Jews for their existing social crises, such as poverty, unemployment, and loss of spiritual direction, Arab leaders *created* the crisis for which they blamed the Jews. In denying the partition of Palestine, Arab governments also refused to allow the resettlement of the Palestinians, so that they could create perpetual evidence of Jewish iniquity: "The refugees are the cornerstone in the Arab struggle against Israel. The refugees are the armaments of the Arabs and Arab nationalism." Arab rulers refused to absorb or to resettle the refugees "because it meant the final disposal of a moral asset."[57] Israel could be charged for the suffering of Palestinians only as long as their suffering could be sustained.

The universal refugee crisis is one of the most disturbing and pervasive phenomena of the modern period. Having fled with my family to North America as a stateless refugee (the ship that brought us from Lisbon to New York in 1940 was torpedoed on its return voyage), I know the brunt of involuntary displacement, which almost inevitably involves the deaths of sick and aged relatives, loss of possessions, language, and culture, interrupted schooling and careers, hardships never forgotten or compensated. Palestinian Arabs are to be pitied along with the tens of millions of refugees of the twentieth century. But Palestinians are doubly unfortunate because theirs is the only such displacement that is prolonged for political advantage. Originally, the Palestinians who fled from their homes in 1948 were a relatively small and easily assimilable group, moving often no more than several miles among people who spoke their language and shared their religion and culture. Leaving aside the refugees of the two world wars, as well as Jews driven from Arab lands in numbers equal to the Arabs who fled from Israel, the two massive conflicts that framed Israel's War of Independence— India's war over the creation of Pakistan in 1947 and the Korean War of 1950–53—produced more than 20 million refugees between them, yet most of those refugees were reabsorbed within a generation. Only in the Arab case did a coalition of rulers, with millions of square miles and great wealth at their disposal, foster and cultivate the state of emergency as a means of sustaining a casus belli.

To these four "enhancements" of Arab anti-Zionism over European anti-Semitism may be added a fifth: the Arabs' conscription of the United Nations in perpetuating the Palestinian crisis. Unwilling to expel the Arab states for violating its charter, or to otherwise punish them for the consequences of their aggression against Israel, the UN undertook to administer the Relief and Works Agency (UNRWA), under which the original half million Arab refugees are said to have multiplied eightfold. The UN did not assess Arab states for their upkeep, did not facilitate their absorption into the Arab world, and failed to create the infrastructure for independent self-government. (The Arab League contributed less than Israel to the resettlement of *Arab* refugees.) In this unique instance, the UNHCR (High Commissioner for Refugees) defined as refugees the descendants of refugees. By this measure, Israel now has 3,000,000 Jewish refugees from Arab lands, except that Israel did everything to absorb these citizens rather than exacerbate their misery. Among Arab states, only Jordan offered Palestinian Arabs a form of citizenship as part of its plan to (illegally) annex the West Bank, while other Arab countries allowed them only temporary residence. Until recently, according to its Web site, UNRWA— the Palestinian "welfare state in exile"—employed some 25,000 staff to provide education, health care, social services, and emergency aid to the refugees in Gaza, the West Bank, Jordan, Lebanon, and Syria.[58] Through this and other means, Arab governments turned the United Nations into their ally against Israel.

Anti-Zionism's Effects on the Jews

Hearing the news of a suicide bombing at a Tel Aviv café, a woman calls her cousins to see if they are okay. The Tel Aviv mother replies that the family is shaken, but intact.

"And Anat?" says the woman, asking after the teenager who used to hang out at the detonated café.

"Oh, no worries there," the mother replies. "Anat is at Auschwitz."

Hilarious to Israelis, this joke is unlikely to go over as well with outsiders who don't regularly experience suicide bombings or know that many Israeli high school students visit the German death camp in Poland as part of their education. To the rest of the world, Auschwitz remains the acme of horrors. Israelis, however, find in yesterday's slaughter-ground a refuge from today's.

Although the Arab League could not prevent the creation of a Jewish state, its permanent war against Israel denied Jews one of the main fruits of victory. Liberal democracy is founded on the principle of equal rights, the notion that human beings possess inalienable rights, not as a reward for their achievements but as a function of their human nature. The innovative feature of emancipation was its requirement that such rights be granted rather than earned. With the emergence of modern nation-states, the same principle of rights was extended to the idea of world government. A government of governments would settle disputes through negotiation and diplomacy, requiring as a first principle that all nations be considered equally legitimate. Jews could no more win their equal rights as a people in the international arena than Dreyfus in France or Lilienblum in Russia could have *earned* his rights as a citizen. Whatever else Zionists may have intended when they spoke of "normalizing" the Jewish condition, they could only attain an unexceptional standing among the nations if Israel was treated as every other emerging nation.

This did not happen, any more than emancipation regularized the political status of the Jews in Europe, and for the same reason—that those opposed to such toleration accused Jews of exploiting it for their advantage. The "Arab-Israel conflict" did not turn out to be—as so many people still pretend it is—a normal territorial dispute between two claimants to the same land. Rather, the Arab war against Israel is an asymmetrical attack by the Arab-Islamic world on the *idea* of a Jewish homeland. The Jews' political strategy of accommodation confronts a political tradition of conquest and expansion; a self-defined minority seeks tolerance from a majority bent on hegemonic rule. Arab rejection of Israel rendered the Jews exceptional despite their political self-transformation, for they had no way of extracting the recognition that was theirs by right.

This setback affected the Jews in contradictory ways, most obviously by forcing them to develop what many believe is the strongest military force in the Middle East and the resources needed for national defense: keen operational intelligence, a flexible citizen army, a military-industrial complex, and the technicians, scientists, and inventors to keep it competitive. Soon after the War of Independence, Israel's Defense Forces set up a Science Corps to develop armaments and technologies unavailable from abroad. From this grew a high-tech industry that ranks among the best and largest in the world. Israel pioneered nuclear research out of the same need for defensive capability. "The 100th smallest country with less than 1/1000th of the world's population" has more start-up companies than any country other than the United States and ranks second in venture capital funds and third after the United States and Canada in companies listed on NASDAQ.[59] Israel may have the highest percentage of engineers in the world, 135 per 10,000 persons as opposed to 85 per 10,000 in the United States. The historian Gershom Scholem, when asked why Israel was producing more generals than men of culture, said that Jews were a very talented people and talent goes where it is needed.[60]

As Arab hostility determined the direction of Jewish talent, Jews in Israel followed the time-tested habit of trying to turn their liabilities to advantages. The IDF became the main force for integrating and educating newcomers from many countries, instilling in them civic discipline and a sense of belonging and helping to forge a common culture among diverse constituencies and ethnic groups. Conscripting men and women at the ages of courtship, it was also credited as the country's chief matchmaker. The concept of "purity of arms" in the IDF code of conduct required servicemen and women to "maintain their humanity even during combat." The stated demand for "tenacity of purpose in performing missions and drive to victory" was rendered almost superfluous by the proximity of the battlefield to home.

Israelis had no wish to become "the fist of the Jewish people," as a Tel Aviv friend of mine ruefully put it, much less the fighting front line of the entire democratic world. *Ein breira* became a national byword—"there is no choice [but to prevail]." Dictators and terrorists delight in parading their might: *vide* the military pageants of Iran, North Korea, and Hezbollah. Sovereign nations take pride in exhibiting their armed forces. But Israel invites its visiting foreign dignitaries to tour its Holocaust memorial, as if to say, *All we want is to be spared this fate.*

In the spring of 1967, the specter of the Holocaust rose for the Jews a second time. The Soviets had poured weapons into their client states, Egypt and Syria. Terrorists of the recently constituted Palestine Liberation Organization regularly attacked Israeli civilians from Jordan's West Bank. On May 16, President Gamal Nasser of Egypt ordered the United Nations forces out of the Sinai and began concentrating troops and tanks on the southern border with Israel. A week later he closed the Straits of Tiran to Israeli shipping. Jordan signed on to the military alliance that already existed between Egypt and Syria. The United States warned Israel not to launch any preemptive strike.[61] The city of Montreal where I then lived had just opened a Universal and International EXPO, expecting to lure some 50 million visitors with visions of the glorious future. From Jewish friends in London, Capetown, and Jerusalem I received almost identical messages: "For a change we know just what you're feeling because we are all at the edge of the same precipice." A common anxiety had forged a fairly unified resistance to

Arab aggression—not a complete accord, but as close to one as the Jewish people ever reached on any political issue.[62]

So the relief was giddying when Israel waged a storybook war and in six heady days gained back territory it had lost in 1948, as well as the Sinai Peninsula, the West Bank of the Jordan, and the Golan Heights, from which Syria had been shelling its farmers. Opinion polls taken at the time showed that the majority of Israelis were prepared to trade back most of the land for the long-sought peace, on the assumption that their "victory" had finally given them some bartering leverage over the defeated parties. But Arab leaders did not act as the defeated parties. Egypt's President Nasser opened a new front against Israel along the Suez Canal, declaring, "If the enemy [Israel] succeeds in inflicting 50,000 casualties in this campaign, we can go on fighting nevertheless, because we have manpower reserves. If we succeed in inflicting 10,000 casualties, he will unavoidably find himself compelled to stop fighting, because he has no manpower reserves."[63]

The Six Days' War brought about the very opposite of the triumphalism that so many later claimed for it. The Arabs did not acknowledge defeat. They followed up the Six Days' War with the War of Attrition along the Suez Canal and the Yom Kippur War of 1973. The Palestinian terrorists who were expelled by the thousands from Jordan established new bases in Lebanon, funded by Arab rulers who wanted to maintain militias for which they could not be held politically accountable.

By far the most significant achievement of the Pan-Arab coalition was the enactment at the United Nations of Resolution 3379 (by a vote of 72 to 35 with 32 abstentions), determining that "Zionism is a form of racism and racial discrimination." Henceforth, Jews could be blamed for the racist discrimination that was being practiced against them. Having earned the right to defend themselves, Israelis discovered that they were now burdened with perpetual self-defense.

Neither had Israel's impressive victories affected the region's radical imbalance of power. No other country, and certainly no other democracy, had ever faced so lopsided a set of adversaries. The growing oil wealth and demographic advantage of the Arab world allowed its rulers to press their political advantages virtually without fear of retribution. The fusion of nationalism with Islam became ever more toxic. In the 1930s, King Abd al Aziz ibn Saud had informed a British visitor to his court: "Verily, the word of God teaches us, and we implicitly believe it, that for a Muslim to kill a Jew, or for him to be killed by a Jew, ensures him an immediate entry into Heaven and into the august presence of God Almighty."[64] By the end of the century, Muslim clerics were disseminating a full-scale program of genocide in the name of Allah and the Koran. This is one of many such sermons by Dr. Mahmoud Mustafah Najem:

Allah described [Jews] in His Book, characterized by conceit, pride, arrogance, rampage, disloyalty and treachery . . . deceit and cunning . . . for which Allah transformed them to monkeys and pigs.

They are guilty of trickery, plotting and treachery, and ideological terrorism . . .

They coveted, and they covet still. They killed, and they kill still. They betrayed, and betray still. They spilled blood, and they spill blood still . . .

We shall battle them and wage Jihad against them . . .

Allah loves those who battle for Him in one line . . .

Oh, servants of Allah, be you the ones by whom Allah tortures the Jews with harsh torment . . .

Allah render us victorious over the devils and demons and over our submission to them . . .

Allah render us victorious over the Jews and those who side with them!

Allah render us victorious over the Jews and those who side with them!

Allah render us victorious over the Jews and the patrons of their arrogance!

Allah unite our ranks and raise our flag!

Allah render victory upon Islam and Muslims! [Abridged][65]

Whereas Christians had berated Jews for not adhering to the moral standards they imposed equally on themselves, Muslim clerics did not hesitate to cite self-chastising sections of the Torah as justification for Allah's plan to annihilate the Jews. They treated Jewish self-criticism as weakness, and scorned a culture that confessed its misdeeds.

Jews were required to assess as never before the strategic options available to them on the home front, in their region, and in the family of nations. Whom could they hope to enlist as allies in their asymmetrical struggle? What defensive boundaries would provide the greatest security for their citizens? How could they expose Arab exploitation of the Palestinian refugee crisis and coerce the Palestinians into building rather than destroying? With what symbols and signs of strength, confidence, determination, and power could they convince the Arab and Muslim world that the disposition of Israel was not negotiable? How could Arab propaganda be neutralized or thwarted? How could Israel's achievement be shown off to best advantage? How could the Jewish spirit inspirit a dispirited world? Now that the Jews were a nation with a land, a national government, and means of self-defense, what could they learn from their past that would help them negotiate through exceedingly narrow straits?

Two opposite movements arose in Israel in response to the political impasse—Gush Emunim, the Bloc of the Faithful, and Shalom Achshav, Peace Now. Neither of them articulated the unique political dilemma facing their country or developed a strategic plan of national defense. The Gush proposed to annex once and for all the disputed territories of Israel up to the natural boundary of the Jordan River; Peace Now, to return of most of the disputed territories on the grounds that their sizable Arab populations would otherwise prolong the conflict. Gush Emunim cast its project as a religious obligation, claiming that the disputed lands were part of the Jews' biblical inheritance. Shalom Achshav insisted that unilateral concession of the territories would result in regional "peace." The first group professed to satisfy the will of God, the second, the will of the Arabs. The first assertion was not subject to proof, and the second was demonstrably bogus. The West Bank had been in Jordan's hands before the combined Arab attacks on Israel. One could legitimately argue for strategic withdrawal from the captured territories on defensive grounds, but there could be no expectation of peace in a return to status quo ante. Since the disputed territories were Israel's as a *result* of Arab aggression, they could not retroactively have become its *cause*.

As Arab hostility against Israel became more protean and voluble, using the United Nations as its international pulpit, the debate within Israel between the "nationalist-religious" and "peace" camps proved eerily reminiscent of the politics in the country two thousand years earlier. That the strongest, though by no means only, champions of retaining and settling at least part of the disputed territories were religious Jews (their knitted skullcap—*kipa sruga*—became a byword for modern Zionist orthodoxy in Israel) allowed the so-called Peace Camp to characterize its opponents as "zealots." The absence of any corresponding peace drive in the Arab world did not prevent the Israeli progressive camp from blaming hostilities on their "intransigent" fellow Jews.

The anger of Israeli elites against the more militant of

their fellow citizens escalated in 1977, when the Labor Party for the first time since the creation of Israel lost control of government to the rival Likud—the much altered but still recognizable party of the Revisionist Israeli Right. In the aftermath of that election, Meron Benvenisti, who had developed a special relationship with the Arab population during the several years he served as deputy major of Jerusalem, recalled traveling on a Haifa bus and looking around at his fellow Jewish passengers with contempt and indifference—"almost as lower forms of human life."[66] It became fashionable in the liberal media to claim that peace would break out were it not for the Israeli "occupation." The Pan-Arab war against the Jews was obscured and displaced by focus on Israeli wrongdoing. The political Left revived the slogans of the 1930s charging Israel with imperialist expansion. State departments and businessmen with an eye on Arab oil and Muslim markets found it convenient to blame Israel for Arab aggression against it. Following two suicide bombings by Hamas in 1995 (one of whose victims was Aliza Flatow of New Jersey), Israel's most prominent writer, Amos Oz, appeared in the *New York Times* to accuse Likud for engendering an atmosphere of "religious, chauvinistic egoism" that benefited from Arab violence and replicated its extremism.[67]

The usual protest against such analogies between Hamas and Likud, or between Arab aggressors and Israeli defenders, is that they create a false *moral* equivalence between the instigators of hostility and those required to guard against it. Some monitors of "honest reporting" point out that "though not all Arabs are haters and not every Israeli is a paragon of tolerance, there is simply no comparison between what goes on in terms of learning about peace and hate between Israel and its Arab neighbors."[68] Well intentioned as such distinctions may be, it is the phony *political* rather than moral equivalence between a culture of blame and a politics of accommodation that stands in the way of grasping what is at stake in the Middle East. Moral standards are subject to interpretation, political contrasts are manifest in deeds. When Muslims argue that Allah commands them to "torture the Jews with harsh torment" as part of their righteous jihad against Israel, they may be no less convinced of their moral rectitude than Western pacifists. The polities of Arabs and Jews are set on a collision course because of their asymmetrical traditions of conquest and accommodation, irrespective of what moral valence one ascribes to each.

Obeying their instinct for survival, most members of Peace Now and the Israeli elites did not interrupt their military service while they lobbied in Washington for a Palestinian state and otherwise promoted their enemies' cause over their own. When all was said and done, they were not prepared to sacrifice their children, their parents, or their country to their imaginary "partners for peace." The dissonance between what they knew to be true and what they wished to be true induced a perpetual tension between their words and actions. If hypocrisy is to profess a principle that you don't abide by, as when rabbis commit adultery or priests steal from the collection plate, Israeli elites practiced hypocrisy in reverse—abiding by principles that they would not profess. Reluctant warriors, they sought relief off the battlefield from the battles they felt compelled to wage. They did not dissuade their children from joining the paratroopers, or pretend that an army desk job equaled service in *krav*—in the field. They may have turned Zionism—*tsiyonut*—into a byword for cant, for empty and tiresome phraseology, but they continued to live out, and often to live out passionately, the Zionist reality they would not preach.

In this respect, Israeli "peacenik-combatants" were utterly unlike the American draft resisters of the anti–Vietnam War movement who burned their draft notices and refused to fight in a war they opposed. Although the two situations were often compared, Israelis were not fighting a foreign war, but for their country that had been attacked from birth.

. . . Its Effect on the Arabs

November 19, 1977, was a rare moment in the history of the modern Middle East. "As if a messenger from Allah had descended to the Promised Land on a magic carpet," the president of Egypt, Anwar Sadat, landed at Ben Gurion airport to be greeted by Israel's past and present leaders.[69] The next day, thousands of Israelis cheered Sadat as he made his way to the Israeli parliament, the Knesset, to address the nation. The Israeli Hebrew press ran Arabic headlines to welcome the visitor, soccer fans proposed Israeli-Egyptian matches, Israeli radio played Egyptian music. The people of Israel "fell in love with the enemy."[70] For once, anti-Jewish hostility seemed to have been arrested before its goal had been achieved.

The euphoria was short-lived. Prime Minister Begin's return visit to Cairo the following month might have occurred on a different planet. In Egypt there were no cheering mobs, no Israeli flags, and no signs of welcome. Sadat sent a deputy in his stead to greet the Israeli head of state. Defense Minister Ezer Weizman noted the "chilly reception, the indifference toward Begin, the flouting of the most elementary rules of protocol and courtesy."[71] Israel had inverted the roles of victor and vanquished by giving Sadat a conquering hero's welcome, without heeding his words: "You should clearly understand the lesson of confrontation between you and us. Expansion does not pay. To speak frankly, our land does not yield itself to bargaining, it is not even open to argument. . . . We cannot accept any attempt to take away one inch of it nor can we accept the principle of debating or bargaining over it."[72] Israel's drive for peace came up against the Arabs' desire to drive Israel from the region. In the ensuing negotiations at Camp David, the supposedly intransigent right-wing prime minister Menahem Begin yielded every last inch of the captured Sinai and uprooted the already thriving Jewish settlements to satisfy the demands of the reputedly conciliatory Anwar Sadat for a *Judenrein* Sinai—a territory absolutely cleared of every last Jew.

During their meeting, former Israeli prime minister Golda Meir reportedly told Sadat, "We can forgive you for killing our sons. But we will never forgive you for making us kill yours." Her chiasmus—a type of rhetorical balance in which the second part reverses the terms of the first—subordinated the pain of losing soldiers to the pain of having to soldier. This point had been made long before by the foremost exegete Rashi (Rabbi Shlomo Yitzhaki, 1040–1105) in his commentary on the passage of Genesis 32:4: *Va'yira yaakov m'od*, Jacob was very afraid, *Va'yey'tzer lo*, and he was greatly distressed. Rashi explains that Jacob was "very afraid" lest he be killed by his brother Esau, but he was even more "distressed" that, in self-defense, he might have to kill Esau.[73] Whereas Rashi was expounding this high moral principle for his Jewish audience, Golda Meir was admitting it to an antagonist whose political traditions interpreted her confession as weakness. Like the Warsaw mother with whom this book began who instructed her son to be a *mentsh*, with her words Golda expressed more concern with Israeli children's decency than with her enemies' designs on them. She would have demonstrated greater understanding of her Egyptian counterpart and greater appreciation of political reality had she asked Sadat to convey to his people the message "We Jews are here to stay," requiring decency, tolerance, and realism of *them*.

Nothing should detract from Anwar Sadat's courage in

providing a new model of Arab leadership or from his diplomatic skills in negotiating with the Israelis. But his conscience was formed by an opposite political tradition and
functioned in an opposite political climate. Four years earlier, when Golda Meir had been prime minister, he had coordinated with Syria the attack on Yom Kippur, the holiest day
of the Jewish year. If he now came to Jerusalem to regain
the territories lost by Egypt, it was not out of regret for
having killed too many Jews but with the realization that he
could not kill enough to defeat them. His efforts to charm
the Israeli public stood in starkest contrast to his failure to
warm his own public to the prospects for peace. And, of
course, he had much to fear. Hostilities against Israel remained so fundamental to Arab unity that the Arab League
suspended Egypt when President Sadat signed the peace
treaty with Israel, moving its headquarters from Cairo to
Tunis. Sadat was assassinated two years later. By the time
the Arab League moved its headquarters back to Cairo in
1989, Egypt had reclaimed its status by breaking almost
every condition of the peace treaty with Israel it had undertaken to implement.

Sadat's initiative hardened anti-Zionism in the rest of the
Arab world. The alliance between the Arab and Communist
blocs that fueled some of the anti-Israel belligerence also
provided the Arab Left with an ideological language far more
potent than the anti-Semitism of the Right. It was under
Soviet tutelage that Arabs adopted the Soviet anti-Zionist
slogans of the 1930s, substituting "racist" for "imperialist"

as the updated term of abuse. Palestinian terrorist leaders were coached by Soviet intelligence agencies and educated at Soviet universities. Mahmoud Abbas, the first elected prime minister of the Palestinian Authority, received his PhD from the Peoples Friendship University in Moscow for a dissertation on "secret relations between Nazism and the leadership of the Zionist movement," in which he argued that Zionists encouraged Nazism in order to gain sympathies for Jewish immigration to Palestine, and that after the war, with the same purpose, Zionists vastly inflated the number of Jewish Holocaust victims.[74] One asks in vain what might have been the fate of Palestinians had Abbas and his generation of Arab leaders been studying how to improve education, health care, governance, trade and commerce, and public works— had they prepared themselves to build their own societies rather than destroying someone else's.

. . . Its Creation of Surrogate Jews

Palestinian Arabs are hardly blind to the ways they have been exploited in the war against Israel. One rueful Arab refugee of 1948 compared the hospitable welcome Palestinians used to offer other Arab immigrants with the cold shoulder *they* were given when they left Israel. He deplored the absence of any public movement in the Arab world to provide welfare services to the refugees.[75] Yet when it came to ascribing blame for their condition, most Palestinians followed their leaders in reproaching Israel and the Jews rather than the Arab governments that kept them homeless. Assigned the role of contesting Israel, and indulged by their fellow Arabs only to the extent that they fulfilled that function, Palestinians, once said to be the most highly accomplished in the Arab world, forged their identity to an unprecedented degree in obsessive opposition to another people.

The theorist of Palestinian nationalism Rashid Khalidi compares Palestinians to Kurds and Armenians, two peoples that have a "clearly defined sense of national identity but have long failed to achieve national independence."[76] But his comparison reveals more differences than similarities. Kurds are a people of Indo-European origin with their own language, traditions, and culture. Armenian communities, dating from long before the Christian era, likewise have their own alphabet and language and national customs. Ironically enough, both these ethnically distinct minorities failed to achieve independence largely thanks to Arab and Islamic opposition, and both experienced mass murder at Muslim hands. Palestinians, on the other hand, share the language, religions, customs, and territory of the Arab majority. They form a majority in Jordan, which they consider a natural repository of their national aspirations. The current competition for leadership among Palestinians of Islamist groups like Hamas reflects their fraternal ties to their Islamic coreligionists elsewhere in the Middle East. Had Palestinians not enjoyed the political support of the entire Arab world, they would never have become the only nationalism to be recognized by the United Nations *prior* to statehood.

The special ingredient of Palestinian nationalism that really does set it apart from, say, Jordanian nationalism, or that of Syria or Egypt, is its basis in antagonism to Israel and its usurpation of Jewish symbols, history, and identity. The most important date in the Palestinian calendar is no Muslim, Arab, or native Palestinian commemoration or celebration, but May 14, 1948, the day of Israel's founding. Drawing their images from both the destruction of the Temple and the mass murder of the Jews of Europe, Palestinians commemorate the birthday of Israel as their *nakba*, or cataclysm. They refer to the *nakba* as "Palestine's endless Holocaust," describing the flight of Arabs during Israel's War of Independence in terms that imitate Holocaust commemoration. Web sites offer "survivors' testimonies" and allege "mass deportations," ascribing to Palestinians the role of Jews and to Jews the role of Nazis.[77] A Palestinian calendar that offers up the Palestinian story "from before the British mandate and up to today's Apartheid Wall [*sic*]" contains not a single entry that is independent of Israel.[78] January 7 is Martyr's Day, commemorating the "documented deaths" of Palestinians as a result of Israeli occupation. February 17 highlights "the Lavon Affair," marking the day in 1955 when the Israeli defense minister Lavon was forced to resign after exposure of an Israeli spy ring in Egypt. The entry for Palestinian Mother's Day, March 21, reminds us that tributes of flowers are no longer to be brought to mothers but laid by them on the gravesites of their martyred children. April is the cruelest month: 3 to 12 marks the "massacre of Jenin in 2002" and April 9 the 1948 massacre of Deir Yassin, but by way of compensation, April 16 honors the start of the first "Great" Arab uprising, led by Haj Amin al Husseini (see earlier), anticipating December 9, which the calendar marks as the date of the second—not the first—intifada against Israel in 1987. An *Addams Family* caricature could not do justice to the ghoulish delight this document takes in self-torment, self-pity, self-punishment, and self-destruction at the hands of demon-Israel.

This Palestinian strategy of inversion and usurpation obviously demoralizes Jews, but its greatest damage is surely to the Palestinians themselves. When Jean-Paul Sartre wrote, "If the Jew did not exist, the anti-Semite would invent him," he had in mind the European psychopath who cannot experience his selfhood, let alone his manhood, except in opposition to the Jew.[79] Sartre could scarcely have imagined a people that fashioned its entire identity, its myths and holidays, its symbols and slogans, its domestic and foreign policy, around opposition to the Jews. Likewise, when the political philosopher Leo Strauss wrote in 1962 that the Nazi regime was the only regime he knew of "based on no principle other than the negation of Jews,"[80] he could scarcely have imagined the exclusivity of the Palestinian obsession.

One would never know from Palestinian rhetoric that in 1950, when Jordan controlled both banks of the river, it allocated East and West banks equal representation in its parliament, and that with or without the disputed territories the major part of Palestine is already in Arab hands. The national consciousness of Palestinian Arabs is so politically focused on what belongs to the Jews that they cannot concentrate on what is theirs to enjoy. "Beloved Palestine, how can I live away from your plains and hills," writes a poet from his home in Damascus, scarcely more than an hour's drive from his native Tulkarem.[81] Both these cities are part of the area that Arabs consider Greater Palestine and that Syria still claims as its own. No doubt the author resents the political boundary that now separates Jewish Palestine from the expanses of Arab land, but as he formulates his resentment, he ignores that the contiguous kingdom of Jordan, occupying more than three-quarters of mandate Palestine, actually boasts plains and hills that closely resemble those in neighboring Israel. The ancient sites of Jordan include the capital Amman, and Petra, city of legendary beauty carved out of rock that burns red in the light of the setting sun. Jordan has its equal share of wadis, restorative hot springs, wildlife and nature preserves, historical landmarks, access to the Jordan River and the Dead Sea. Their political orientation makes the vast lands they possess worth less to Arabs than someone else's.

The antithetical politics of Jews and Arabs have produced antithetical results. Through tough centuries, Jews looked inward, caring for one another. Shortly after its founding, Israel passed the Law of Return, granting every Jew the right to immigrate to Israel unless he or she is engaged in an activity directed against the Jewish people or is likely to endanger public health or the security of the state. Under this law, Israel welcomed some of the world's most damaged refugees, providing those who needed it with decades of medical treatment, sustenance, and support. Since Judaism is unique in allowing anyone to become a Jew without insisting that everyone should become a Jew, the Law of Return was a universal immigration law without precedent or equal. Biblical Ruth the Moabite exemplifies the convert, the outsider, who becomes the consummate Jewish insider as ancestress of King David. Panels of Jewish faces in every racial hue that greet visitors to the Museum of the Diaspora in Tel Aviv reflect the multicultural culture of the citizenry. Israel absorbed immigrant groups from Morocco and Ethiopia, Germany and Russia, Argentina and India. The Law of Return is just one of the many ways through which Jews tried to compensate by the highest degree of liberality for the indignities they had suffered in exile. At the same time, non-Jews were also offered Israeli citizenship through other means, including naturalization after a period of residence in the country. Arabic joins Hebrew as an official language of Israel, in deference to its Arab citizens who form about 15 percent of the population.

Predictably, the Law of Return looms on the Palestine calendar for July 15 (1950) as an act of discrimination against Arabs. Because no Arab country shares Israel's sense of responsibility for its co-religionists, because Arabs passed no Law of Return but instead prevented their resettlement,

Palestinians must interpret solidarity as a crime or else admit the crime Arabs committed against them. Zionism's watchword was "We go up to the Land to build and be rebuilt by it." Palestinians call for retributive war. "Some morning we'll return riding the crest of the tide / our bloodied banners fluttering / above the glitter of spears."[82] The Palestinian poet who asks, "How can my poems not turn into guns?" echoes Yasser Arafat's repeated vows to conquer all Palestine through fire and blood.[83] One may sympathize with Palestinians, but it is precisely this sympathy that keeps them hostage to brutish practices.

The Recurring Wish for Reschid Bey

On September 5, 1993, there appeared in the *New York Times* under the banner headline "Promised Land: Israel and the Palestinians See a Way to Co-Exist" an opinion piece that epitomizes the political problem I was provoked into describing in this book. Written by one of America's most celebrated journalists, it heralds the impending Oslo Accords and captures the fevered expectancy of those who were about to celebrate the agreement's signing on the White House lawn:

On Nov. 2 1917 the British Foreign Secretary, Arthur Balfour, issued a declaration in London stating that His Majesty's Government was ready to support the creation of a national home for the Jewish people in Palestine. The Zionist movement took that one paragraph promise, and from it, step by step, erected the state of Israel.

Nearly 76 years later, on Aug. 30 1993, the Israeli Government approved an agreement reached in secret with the Palestine Liberation Organization sanctioning the creation of an autonomous Palestinian homeland in the Gaza Strip and Jericho. This is nothing less than the Israeli Balfour Declaration for the Palestinians, and if they build on it as the Zionists did, there is every chance it will lead to their own state.[84]

Here was Herzl's fantasy of Reschid Bey—Arab created in the image of a Jew—being hailed as a basis for the national policy of Israel. To sustain the make-believe, everything that history had taught since Herzl was being stood on its head. In real life, Jews and Arabs constituted not parallel but politically opposite and contrasting societies. Jews had prepared for a homeland in Palestine long before the Balfour Declaration, and they built on it step by step because it was their habit to exploit any opportunity they were offered to improve their lives. Arab rulers and their terrorist proxies had resisted every opportunity to create the infrastructure for Palestinian independence so as to protect and extend their power. The comparison with Britain was equally loopy. When the vast British Empire of 1917 promised the Jews a homeland, it was acknowledging that many of them had fought loyally under its flag during the First World War. Britain offered the Jews not the West Midlands but some distant possession it was about to cut loose. By contrast, Israel, which is smaller than the Midlands even with the disputed territories, was yielding its own contiguous land to Yasser Arafat, then the world's leading terrorist and founder of the organization dedicated to its destruction.

In fact, seventy-six years after the Balfour Declaration and forty-five years after its Declaration of Independence, Israel was still waiting for the Arabs to recognize *its* right to a homeland. In apparent exhaustion and desperation, it was about to do what no people in human history had ever done—to arm its enemy with the expectation of gaining security. As part of the Oslo agreement placing Arafat in charge of a proto-Palestinian state, Israel was transferring responsibility for combating terror in that territory from its own General Security Service, border police, and military to the PLO, on the assumption that the Palestinian terrorist organization would do a better job of it. Prime Minister Rabin said that he expected his partner to deal with insurrections "without the Supreme Court, without B'tselem [Israel's Human Rights Organization], without some diehard liberals, and without all sorts of mothers and fathers,"[85] ignoring that a partner without any such moral inhibitions would not hesitate to break agreements with *him*.

In the fictional foolstown of Chelm, which figures prominently in Jewish folklore, Jews are always coming up with theoretical proposals—catching the moon in a barrel, carry-

ing the messenger on his rounds so that he should not leave
tracks in the fresh snow—that point up their impracticality.
The Jews of Israel were not the people of Chelm. In 1992
they elected Yitzhak Rabin their prime minister on a plat-
form of national resolve echoing the policy of his predecessor, Yitzhak Shamir, that there would be no negotiations
with the PLO terrorists, no Palestinian state under PLO
supervision, and no political division of Jerusalem. Skirting
the democratic procedures of their country, several rene-
gade Israelis who were funded by Jewish donors overseas met
in secret with PLO leaders to assure them that Israel would
acquiesce to the very ideas its voters rejected. Both parties
to these negotiations were proud enough of their achievements (in the case of the PLO, deservedly so) to leave abun-
dant records of their meetings so that anyone wishing to
unravel the Oslo process can study after the fact what was
concealed from the public and the Israeli government as it
was unfolding.[86] Ultimately, the Israeli government signed
on to the plan that was developed at Oslo, the United States
(and the *New York Times*) gave it its blessing, and the Nobel
Peace Committee awarded its prize to the signatories, leaving local populations to pay the price.

Oslo triggered an immediate escalation of terror not
only against Israel but against the West. Arafat's adoring
reception by Western governments—thirteen invitations by
President Clinton alone—crowned by his installation as
head of the proto-Palestinian state, demonstrated beyond a
doubt the efficacy of terror as the means of getting the bet-

ter of the otherwise much stronger democracies. "There would have been no resistance in Palestine if not for Oslo," a senior leader of the PLO later acknowledged on Arab television. "Throughout the occupied territories, we could not move a single pistol from one place to another. If not for Oslo, the weapons we got through Oslo . . . if not for the training, the camps, the protection provided by Oslo, and if not for the release of thousands of Palestinian prisoners through Oslo—this Palestinian resistance could not have carried out this great Palestinian Intifada."[87] "We deserve the Qassams and the Katyushas," atoned a correspondent of *Ha'aretz* in the summer of 2006: "We earned it honestly as a nation of gullible fools."[88] Against the better judgment of its citizenry, Israel had been conned into substituting a wish for a possibility.

The capitulation of Oslo was a foreseeable and avoidable political mistake, based on a series of self-delusions that anyone could have—and several did—passionately tried to prevent. Norman Podhoretz wrote in January 1992:

> The plain truth is that the Arab-Israeli conflict has from the beginning been rooted in the refusal of the Arab peoples to accept the existence of a sovereign Jewish state in "their" part of the world, no matter where its boundaries might be drawn and irrespective of what its policies might or might not be. Hence the Palestinian problem cannot be the "key" to that conflict (unless this is a coded way of saying, as the Pales-

tine National Covenant still explicitly does, that the only "solution" would be the establishment of Palestinian control not just over the West Bank and Gaza but over the entire territory now under Jewish sovereignty—i.e., the destruction of Israel).[89]

Podhoretz was merely the strongest of several American critics of a "peace process" destined to provoke greater Palestinian violence and to reignite Pan-Arab and Islamic ambitions. But most American Jews and all too many Israelis, at no one's command but their own, reverted to the Diaspora strategy of accommodation in a situation guaranteed to quicken and prolong the war against them.

CONCLUSION

> Jews probably could have endured in the Diaspora
> had theirs been the only type of political organiza-
> tion in the world. But their political system was not
> basically structured to defend itself against outside
> enemies seeking its annihilation.

This quotation conveys the thesis of my book, except that it was not written about the Jews. Here is its original: "Democracy probably could have endured had it been the only type of political organization in the world. But it was not basically structured to defend itself against outside enemies seeking its annihilation."[90] Taking the measure of the cold war in 1983, when the Soviet Union still controlled Eastern Europe and its Communist affiliates, the French intellectual Jean-François Revel feared that a combination of forces intent on the extinction of democracy was becoming more powerful than those forces bent on keeping it alive. He believed that democracy's strengths, such as its self-criticism and high moral standards, contained the seeds of its destruction when faced with an enemy uninhibited by such scruples. That the implosion of the Soviet Union proved his fears groundless in this instance by no means lessens the value of his insights:

> Democracy is by its very nature turned inward. Its vocation is the patient and realistic improvement of life in a community.

> Democracy tends to ignore, even deny, threats to its existence because it loathes doing what is needed to counter them. It awakens only when the danger becomes deadly, imminent, evident. By then, either there is too little time for it to save itself, or the price of survival has become crushingly high.

> [Democracies are beset by] guilt-producing accusations and intimidation that no other political system has had to tolerate. [91]

Most of Revel's observations about "how democracies perish"—the title and warning of his book—seem tailored to the Jews, who are likewise turned politically inward, beset by "guilt-producing accusations," and tend to ignore, even deny, threats to their existence. Their capacity for accommodation dooms them if they fail to repel their assailants when necessary.

The Contradictions of Jewish Power

The creation of Israel solved the crisis of Jewish dispersion by resurrecting the Jewish homeland. But there were two problems it could not solve. The so-called Jewish problem was in reality the problem of nations that blamed their dysfunction on the Jews. (In 1939, Wyndham Lewis, a modernist painter and writer, admonished his fellow Christians that the "Jewish problem" was not of Jewish making but the result of the character of Christian nations and their hostile attitude toward the Jews.[92]) Just as no Jewish initiative could have solved the German problem that culminated in Nazism, no Israeli initiative could correct "what went wrong" in Arab societies.[93] Jews could only hope to enhance their own security through the avoidance of fatal mistakes and nudge the Arab world to greater maturity by making it clear that Israel was in the region to stay.

The second—internal—problem that could not be alleviated by the creation of Israel alone was the relation of Jews to political power. Zionist thinkers had expected sovereignty to result in political normalization without being able to anticipate the role that a tiny Jewish state might play in the international struggle for power. In trying to withstand the Arab assault, Israelis, Jews, and concerned third parties tripped again and again over the same issue of power that had impeded the development of Jewish political history to begin with. If historians once mistook the absence of sovereignty to mean that Jews stood outside politics, modern students of the problem too often assumed that the resumption of sovereignty guaranteed political parity between Israel and the nations. Jews were said to have reversed their political fortunes once they began governing themselves and an Arab minority in a country of their own. Equating "statehood" with "power," the new experts confused Zionism's potential with its achievement, as if the acquired option of Jewish self-defense had erased Arab advantages of numbers, resources, and land.

This misdiagnosis deepened in 1982 when Israel entered Lebanon to destroy the terrorist bases of the Palestine Liberation Organization. The incursion was seized upon as proof of Israel's offensive as well as defensive capability, as well as its potential corruption as an aggressor state. Observers expressed their concern about the "rapidity with which Jews have moved from powerlessness to power," citing Israel's military capability as a major threat to traditional Jewish values.[94] In an effort to chasten modern Israel, the historian David Biale offered a beguilingly contrarian recital of history, locating "power" in situations of prolonged political dependency and "powerlessness" in situations where Jews tried to rule over themselves. Thus, he considers periods of Jewish sovereignty merely preludes to political defeat: "Ultimately, the victory of the Hasmoneans led to the destruction of the Temple itself." Defeat, on the other hand, leads to advantageous political dependency: "The failure of the revolt against the Romans ultimately led to a greater stability and greater Jewish power."[95] By "stability" Biale means the internal Jewish governance of the rabbis under foreign control; the function of "ultimately" in these judgments is to make Diaspora the preferred condition of Jewish political life because it lacks the anxieties of political self-rule.

Critics like Biale were right to hold Israel accountable for its political actions, some of which have been regrettable, though not necessarily in the ways that they imply. His book is useful as an articulation of something larger, harkening back to the politics of complementarity as though accommodation were part of the moral essence of Judaism itself. In the wake of the First World War, the writer and ethnographer S. An-sky theorized that Jewish folklore differed fundamentally from its Gentile counterparts in its aversion to any kind of physical heroism or strength. "The exclusive motif of Jewish folk-tales is the spiritual [not the material] struggle."[96] Having just witnessed what he called "the destruction of Galician Jewry," An-sky found comfort in the spiritual staying power that he said Jews substituted for the conquests valued by other nations. But An-sky's insight, like Biale's, ignored that premodern Jews ascribed to the Almighty, Lord of the Universe, all the physical prowess that they lacked. No daily reader of the Psalms could underestimate the might of God, whose indignation blazed like fire, who avenged the spilled blood of His servants the Jews and would pay back their enemies sevenfold. The glorification of powerlessness was as antithetical to Judaism as belief in the son of God. Jews did not think themselves powerless in the most meaningful sense: had they not reckoned on ultimate vindication, they could not have claimed to believe in justice—one of the cardinal tenets of Jewish civilization. The power of God, emphatically including his eventual action in history, was the guarantee that justice would ultimately triumph. Lacking such faith in God's intervention, modern Jews could not claim to be moral unless they themselves intended to supply the missing dimension of power. Otherwise, they were signing Jews up for a suicide pact with every new set of enemies.

Sovereign Israel was obviously abler to defend itself than were Jewish polities of the Diaspora. However, representations of Israel as a dominant regional *power* replicated its distorted image in the mind of its enemies. Most of the Arab world remains formally in a state of war against Israel. An estimated 13 million Jews worldwide, about 4.5 million fewer than in 1939, try to win tolerance from more than 250 million Arabs, who have ties to more than 1 billion Muslims. Advances in Arab missile technology bring Israel ever more dangerously into enemy sights, while Israel's power remains hugely constrained by international pressure and by its own disinclination to fight those from whom it seeks acceptance.

It would have been strange, indeed, had Jews within decades of recovering their sovereignty reversed the political patterns of millennia to the point of "abusing power" rather than, as had previously been the case, failing at self-protection. Political theory might then have hypothesized that sovereignty itself, independent of political culture or institutions, begets aggression in the very act of declaring independence. Perhaps claims about Israel's political turn-about are governed by some such assumption about the inherent militarism of nation-states, but the behavior of Israel belies any such conclusion. Far from exposing Jews to the temptations of might, the creation of Israel had inadvertently reproduced in the Middle East a political imbalance almost identical to the one that Jews had experienced in the Diaspora. Israelis were no more inclined or able to subdue the Arabs than the nations among whom Jews had sojourned in exile. What Conor Cruise O'Brien called "the siege"—Israel's geopolitical situation from the moment of its founding—restricted the political options of the sovereign Jewish state not much less than statelessness had previously impinged on the Jews of Europe.[97]

Wielding military strength, Israel changed the Jewish political equilibrium in contradictory ways. The options of self-defense that Israel acquired by establishing its own military and intelligence made Jews for the first time in two thousand years a potentially valuable ally, including of the world's superpower, the United States. At the same time, Israel's susceptibility as a Jewish and democratic state greatly enhanced its utility as a political target for those who demonized both Jews and democracy. These advantages and liabilities were inextricably linked, greatly magnifying Israel's prominence in the international arena and exaggerating the image of Jewish "power" without altering the radical imbalance between Arabs and Muslims on one side and Jews on the other. Already the world's most mythologized people, Jews acquired as the despised "Zionist entity" an international reputation greater than Jehovah's.

The Definitive Ally

Israel's political predicament returns us to the place where this book began: Shmuel Zygelboym failed to enlist the help of Allied leaders in 1943 because they did not think that rescuing the Jews was essential to winning the war. He appealed to them on humanitarian grounds, and they felt that they could best serve humanity by defeating Hitler. The British Foreign Office resented the "inconvenience" caused by European Jewry, and even Prime Minister Churchill, who was genuinely moved by the Jews' plight, did not want his intervention on their behalf to jeopardize the rest of the war effort.[98] President Roosevelt likewise tried not to offend the protectionist and isolationist factions in Congress and the State Department. Whatever private sympathies these two great leaders harbored for the Jewish victims— and by reliable accounts, both wanted to do more in the way of rescue than they felt was politically feasible—they did not think of the Jews as political allies, hence they did not reckon Nazi actions against the Jews as part of the war against *them*. Although Great Britain and the United States had joined a war that was already being fought against the

Jews of Europe, they did not think anti-Semitism had a direct bearing on the war they were waging.

Likewise, most Americans never fully grasped the connection between what the historian Lucy Dawidowicz called "the war against the Jews" and Franklin Delano Roosevelt's declaration of war against Germany in December 1941. Opponents of America's entry into the war even cited that connection as a reason for *not* intervening. They said Roosevelt, father of the "Jew Deal," had been pressured by the Jews into joining *their* fight. Yet nothing was further from the truth: even after he had been given incontrovertible evidence of the mass murder of Jews, Roosevelt did not allow the exigency of rescue to distract him from winning the war. Intent on fighting through to an unconditional surrender, he did not want "to divide the American people over what the war in Europe was really about—especially when it was not yet certain that the Allies would win the war in Europe."[99] It is fairer to say that Roosevelt went to war despite seeming to enter it on the side of the Jews. He did not choose to fight for the Jews but was provoked into fighting against the anti-Jews.

In our own day, George Walker Bush was provoked by the Al Qaeda attacks of September 11, 2001, into joining what he called a "war on terror" that had long been waged by radical Arabs and Muslims against the Jews of Israel. Just as before, isolationists like Pat Buchanan accused President Bush of having been manipulated by Jews into joining *their* fight. Buchanan charged American Jews with "deliberately damaging U.S. relations with every state in the Arab world that defies Israel or supports the Palestinian people's right to a homeland of their own." He said that "through their arrogance, hubris, and bellicosity," the Jews had alienated American allies all over the Islamic and Western world, and he insisted that America could have avoided the conflict by courting the Arabs rather than siding with Israel.[100]

Like the isolationists of World War II, Buchanan had it backwards: no more than President Roosevelt did George W. Bush have the Jews in mind when he determined to go to war against those who attacked his country and those who harbored the terrorists. The coordinated strikes against the centers and symbols of American power were aimed at the most powerful democracy in the world: Israel figured merely the "little Satan" as compared to the "big," the more accessible and vulnerable target in an escalating struggle. But this time—unlike in World War II—some officials recognized the correspondence between the two conflicts. "We are all Jews now," declared James Woolsey, former director of the CIA, spelling out the logic of the Bush administration's foreign policy in the wake of 9/11: "We should all reflect upon the historic reality that when anti-Semitism raises its head, the rest of us, unless we are willing to live with a foot on our necks will be the next targets."[101] Though President Bush did not go to war to help the Jews, like Roosevelt, he was provoked into fighting the anti-Jews.

In 1943 the Dutch-born journalist-writer Pierre Van Paassen tried to stir the British conscience with an account of the help they were receiving from their "forgotten ally," the Jews of Palestine.[102] He excoriated the British for sacrificing the Jews fighting on their behalf in order to gain the support of Arab leaders fighting against them. At present, many Americans and most members of Congress need no such reminder. They are persuaded that Israel is, along with Britain and Australia, the strongest ally of the United States, and certainly the most tested in battle. Americans combating terror routinely learn from Israel's experience and rely on Israeli expertise in everything from airport security to trauma relief. The administration of George W. Bush articulated more clearly than any of its predecessors the strategic connection between Israel's security and its own. This, then, is the greatest difference for the Jews since the founding of Israel—that they have something to offer as an acknowledged ally, not merely as individual Jews behind the scenes, as bankers or scientists, cultural creators or impresarios, but collectively, because of the political role they have been forced to play. For the first time, the ability of Jews to withstand their assailants affects the security of other nations as much as their own. Jews always believed that they were meant to help repair the world, but now that belief has turned into plain political fact, albeit in the form they least expected and least desired.

Many liberal supporters of Israel are disheartened by how little the resumption of Jewish statehood has affected the political standing of Jews among the nations, and by the new hostility it awakened. Zionists had correctly identified the variable of statelessness as a cause of anti-Semitism, but in returning to the Land of Israel, Jews could not escape the further predicament of their merit. For many centuries Christians had tried to stick Jews with the bill for the Bible they had appropriated from them. One theory held that Christians hated the Jews for saddling them with Christianity itself. Now Muslims, in direst need of an explanation for their slippage in world historical standing, try to pin their collapse on Jewish accomplishment. As the politics of blame reaches its apotheosis in opposition to the Jewish state, Jews are called on to muster more creative resistance than had ever been demanded of them or of any other people.

But if changes in the Jewish polity had left it more exposed, Israel had also acquired strategic and principled significance. As the only regional democracy with a constitutional culture strong enough to sustain its political structure, Israel is a crucially situated outpost of the West. Easier to attack than the larger democracies of Europe and the Americas, Israel was now inextricably linked to their defense. To ignore threats to Israel's existence is to invite earlier attacks on one's own.

There was a time when autocrats risked little or nothing by sacrificing their Jews to invaders or mobs. If threatened, the Gentile master could throw the dog a Jewish bone to deflect it from his own juicier thigh. The attackers might be satisfied with the bone, or choke on it. Or else the master himself—England's Edward I leaps to mind—would drain the Jews of their money and possessions, execute their leaders, and expel the rest.

Democracies do not enjoy the same impunity when it comes to sacrificing their Jews. Democratic leaders may still try to appease a restive underclass the way the French government tends to let Arab gangs target Jews as a limited, presumably harmless outlet for frustration, or the way British elites try to appease Muslims by joining in anti-Israel agitation. But far from choking on the Jewish bone, aggressors against a democratic system are more often invigorated by their anti-Semitism to move against society as a whole. Jews in democratic societies are not merely the proverbial canaries sent into the mine shaft to test the quality of the air: they function rather as the kindling used to set the system aflame. Why stop at the Jews? Thugs who get away with harassing Jewish citizens go on to torch the rest of the citizenry.

So, too, when Israel is assaulted in the international arena, its fellow democracies may prefer to remain neutral rather than risk alienating the assailants, reluctant to subordinate their self-interest to the defense of a foreign nation. Self-styled political "realists" argue that if Israel is a liability it should be sacrificed to American priorities in the hope that the Arab-Muslim consortium targeting the Jews would be satisfied by the prospect of that limited conquest. The record of the United Nations encourages an opposite deduction. Time and again, opposition to Israel has been the vehicle for successful alliances against America and human rights efforts in the rest of the world. In the 1960s, the Arab-Soviet bloc used opposition to Israel to take political control of the world organization for which America was footing most of the bill. Resolutions attacking Israel's "racism" and "discrimination" routinely divert attention from their sponsors, who, unlike Israel, institutionalize racism and discrimination (including against women) in their countries. An astute young German, Sebastian Haffner, noted that the Nazis came to power by provoking a general discussion "not about their own existence, but about the right of their victims to exist."[103] By the same technique, assaults on Israel's legitimacy obscure the abuses of the countries that are pointing the finger. Professional observers have by now provided ample evidence of how the Arab war against Israel "debased the UN, sullied its charter, perverted the meaning of human rights, and ransacked international law and its highest Court."[104]

Prospects for peace in our time depend on how soon Israel is granted the unexceptional place it earned in the family of nations. This outcome hangs on two factors—whether Arab and Muslim leaders and populations can be persuaded by word and deed to drop Israel from their political agenda, and, until that happens, whether Israel and world Jewry have the staying power to repel the Arab assault. The word goes forth from Zion in ways that earlier Israelites never intended: in defending themselves, Jews have been turned into the fighting front line of the democratic world.

NOTES

Prologue

1. Itsik Manger, "My Path in Yiddish Literature," in *Shriftn in Proze* [Prose Works] (Tel Aviv: Peretz Farlag, 1980), 362.

Part One

1. Josephus, *The Jewish War*, trans. G. A. Williamson (Harmondsworth, Middlesex, England: Penguin, 1959), 339.

2. Heinrich Graetz, title essay in *The Structure of Jewish History*, trans., ed., and introduced by Ismar Schorsch (New York: Jewish Theological Seminary, 1975), 63–124. Quotations on pp. 70 and 84.

3. Herman Cohen, "Graetz's Philosophy of Jewish History," in Alan L. Mittleman, *The Scepter Shall Not Depart from Judah: Perspectives on the Persistence of the Political in Judaism* (Lanham: Lexington Books, 2000), 35.

4. Simon Dubnow, *Nationalism and History: Essays on Old and New Judaism*, ed. Koppel S. Pinson (Philadelphia: Jewish Publication Society, 1958), 80.

5. Ibid., 99.

6. Leo Pinsker, "Auto-Emancipation: An Appeal to His People by a Russian Jew," trans. David Blondheim, in *The Zionist Idea*, ed. Arthur Hertzberg (Philadelphia: Jewish Publication Society, 1959), 181–98.

7. Bialik, "In the City of Slaughter," trans. A. M. Klein, in David G. Roskies, ed., *The Literature of Destruction: Jewish Responses to Catastrophe* (Philadelphia: The Jewish Publication Society, 1989), 161.

8. Haim Hazaz, "The Sermon," trans. Ben Halpern, in *Modern Hebrew Literature*, ed. Robert Alter (New York: Behrman, 1975), 274.

9. Daniel Elazar, ed., Kinship and Consent: *The Jewish Political Tradition and Its Contemporary Uses* (Ramat Gan, Israel: Turtledove Publishers, 1981), 25.

10. I Kings 5:11. See, e.g., Haim Tadmor, "The United Monarchy," in *A History of the Jewish People*, ed. H. H. Ben-Sasson (Cambridge: Harvard University Press, 1969), 102–6.

11. Jeremiah 10:25. This same sentiment is voiced as part of the Passover seder, just prior to the praise of God for His bounty.

12. Matthew 5:43–48.

13. Bernard Lewis, "Islamic Revolution," *New York Review of Books* 34, no. 21–22 (January 21, 1988).

14. *Tanakh: The Holy Scriptures* (Philadelphia: The Jewish Publication Society, 1985), 1272.

15. St. Augustine of Hippo, *Expositions on the Psalms*.

16. *The Psalms*, commentary A. Cohen (London: Soncino Press, 1945), 447.

17. Yehezkel Kaufman, "The Age of Classical Prophecy," trans. Moshe Greenberg, in *Great Ages and Ideas of the Jewish People*, ed. Leo W. Schwartz (New York: Random House, 1956), 77.

18. Salo Baron, *A Social and Religious History of the Jews*, vol. 1 (New York: Columbia University, 1952), 233.

19. Menahem Stern, "Antisemitism in Rome," in Shmuel Ettinger, *Antisemitism Through the Ages*, ed. Shmuel Almog, trans. Nathan H. Reisner (Oxford, England: Pergamon Press, 1988), 14ff.

20. G. A. Williamson, "Introduction," in Josephus, *The Jewish War*, 14.

21. Josephus, *The Jewish War*, 22.

22. Jeffrey L. Rubenstein, *Talmudic Stories: Narrative Art, Composition, and Culture* (Baltimore: Johns Hopkins University Press, 1999), 148.

23. Hayim Nahman Bialik and Yehoshua Hana Ravnitzky, *The Book of Legends: Sefer Ha-aggadah*, trans. William G. Braude (New York: Schocken Books, 1992), 189.

24. Users of the Internet are invited to Google the words "Kamtza Bar Kamtza" for selective applications of this story to current affairs.

25. Nehemiah 8:2–3. in *Tanakh*, 1519.

26. Avot (Ethics of the Fathers) 1:2. The original reference to Temple service was transposed to synagogue service.

27. "At Home While Abroad" is the second chapter of Isaiah Gafni's valuable study, *Land, Center, and Diaspora: Jewish Constructs in Late Antiquity* (Sheffield, England: Sheffield Academic Press, 1997), 41–57. Of particular interest is the book's final chapter, which shows how the Babylonian community of scholars developed a self-image as the "equivalent" of Eretz Israel (p. 116).

28. The two quoted phrases and some of this interpretation are from Gedaliah Alon, *The Jews in the Land in the Talmudic Age (70–640 CE)*, vol. 1, trans. and ed. Gershon Levi (Jerusalem: Magnes Press, 1980), 95 and 112. See also Jacob Neusner, *First-Century Judaism in Crisis: Yohanan ben Zakkai and the Renaissance of Torah*, augmented ed. (New York: KTAV, 1982).

29. To those who asked, "Is not a landless people like a soul without a body?" Rabbi Yohanan and his followers might have answered, "Certainly it is; and we believe in the survival of the soul." Isidore Epstein, *Judaism* (London: Penguin Books, 1959), 113.

30. Werner Sombart, *The Jews and Modern Capitalism*, trans. Mordecai Epstein (New Brunswick, N.J.: Transaction Books, 1982), 328.

31. Yosef Hayim Yerushalmi, "Exile and Expulsion in Jewish History," in *Crisis and Creativity in the Sephardic World 1391–1648*, ed. Benjamin R. Gampel (New York: Columbia University Press, 1997), 11.

32. Ibid., 14.

33. Jane S. Gerber, *The Jews of Spain: A History of the Sephardic Experience* (New York: Free Press, 1992), 39.

34. The annual *Polin: Studies in Polish Jewry* prefaces its volumes with versions of the legend as cited by Sholem Asch and S. Y. Agnon.

35. Yom Kippur traditional evening service.

36. Sombart, *Jews and Modern Capitalism*, 13.

37. Saul Lieberman, "Response to the Introduction by Professor Alexander Marx" (1948), in *The Jewish Expression*, ed. Judah Goldin (New York: Bantam, 1970), 127–28.

38. Gordon Freeman, "The Rabbinic Understanding of Covenant as a Political Idea," in *Kinship and Consent*, 66.

39. Milton Himmelfarb, "The Jew: Subject or Object?" *Commentary* (July 1965): 55. Also in his selected essays, *The Jews of Modernity* (Philadelphia: Jewish Publication Society, 1973), 240.

40. Menachem Elon, *Jewish Law: History, Sources, Principles*, vol. 2, trans. Bernard Auerbach and Melvin J. Sykes (Philadelphia: Jewish Publication Society, 1994), 680–81.

41. Alan Dowty, "Is There a Jewish Politics?" in *The Role of Domestic Politics in Israeli Peacemaking* (Jerusalem: Leonard Davis Institute for International Relations at the Hebrew University, 1997), 3. See also Alan Dowty, "Israel's First Decade: Building a Civic State," in *Israel: The First Decade*, ed. S. Ilan Troen and Noah Lucas (Albany: State University of New York Press, 1995), 32–36.

42. Himmelfarb, *Jews of Modernity*, 240.

43. Mendele Mocher Sforim, "Of Bygone Days," trans. Raymond Scheindlin, in *A Shtetl and Other Yiddish Novellas*, ed. Ruth R. Wisse (New York, Behrman House, 1973), 273–74.

44. Tractate Bava Batra 8B. For its application to contemporary Jewish politics, see David Golinkin, "Pidyon Shvuyim (The Redemption of Captives): How Far Should Israel Go in Order to Redeem Captives from Terrorist Organizations?" http://www.jewishvirtuallibrary. org/jsource/Judaism/captives.html (Virtual Jewish Library Web site), posted October 2, 2003, by the Schechter Institute of Jewish Studies in Jerusalem.

45. Who can fail to marvel that Jews have garnered almost one quarter of the Nobel Prizes awarded between 1901 and 2004? While the global Islamic population of about 1.2 billion (20 percent of the world's population) generated seven such prizes in the same period (two of them to Anwar Sadat and Yasser Arafat for agreeing or pretending to agree to peace with Israel), the global Jewish population of approximately 13 million (.02 percent of the world's population) collected eight peace prizes, twenty-eight in chemistry, twenty-one in economics, fifty-three in medicine and physiology, and forty-five in physics. I cite these remarkable figures not in the spirit of braggadocio but to probe what the historian Ralph Marcus has called the Jewish "combination of flexibility and inflexibility."

46. E[isig] S[ilberschlag], "Hebrew Literature, Modern," in *Encyclopaedia Judaica*, vol. 8 (Jerusalem: Macmillan, 1971), 176.

47. This formulation is not mine, but I cannot recall its source.

48. Thanks to Wolfhart P. Heinrichs for helping me clarify this.

49. Joshua A. Fishman, *Yiddish: Turning to Life* (Amsterdam: John Benjamins Publishing Company, 1991), 69.

50. Ibid., 27.

51. The Jewish Language Research Web site, ed. Sarah Bunin Benor, keeps updating information that scholars provide.

52. Yiddish itself developed several regional variants, reflecting lines of political separation among European Jewish communities that predated and were independent of the national or natural boundaries that separated the coterritorial languages. A useful introduction to "Jewish languages" can be found in Steven M. Lowenstein's *The Jewish Cultural Tapestry* (New York: Oxford University Press, 2000), 49–67.

53. Max Weinreich, *History of the Yiddish Language*, trans. Shlomo Noble with the assistance of Joshua A. Fishman (Chicago: University of Chicago Press, 1980), 30–31.

54. On a trip to Poland in the 1980s, a couple of Israelis in my group who were native Polish speakers overheard two locals commenting on their conversation, "That's the way they used to speak before the war." The Israelis corrected the men: "Before the war, Jews spoke Yiddish. Just now we were speaking Hebrew." The men responded, "That's the way you used to speak when you didn't want us to understand." They were accurately describing the way Jews would sharply increase the Hebrew component of their Yiddish whenever they wanted to keep things private from non-Jewish neighbors who could be presumed to understand everyday Yiddish.

55. See Nathan Cohen, *Books, Writers, and Newspapers: The Jewish Cultural Center in Warsaw, 1918–1942* (in Hebrew) (Jerusalem: Magnes Press, 2003), 70–74.

56. Moishe Leib Halpern attributes this suggestion to a fictional uncle in "Anti-yiddishism," *Vokh* 21 (New York: March 1930).

57. Eliezer Ben-Yehuda, *A Dream Come True*, trans. T. Muraoka (Boulder, Colo.:Westview Press, 1993), 37.

58. Johann Gottlieb Fichte, "To the German Nation" (1806), *Addresses to the German Nation*, ed. George A. Kelly (New York: Harper Torch Books, 1968), 190–91. See Fourth Address in particular, which focuses on language.

59. Richard Wagner, "Modern," *Bayreuther Blatter* (March 1878), excerpted in ed. Richard S. Levy, *Antisemitism in the Modern World: An Anthology of Texts* (Lexington, Mass.: D.C. Heath, 1991), 52.

60. Steven E. Aschheim, *Brothers and Strangers: The East European Jew in German and German Jewish Consciousness, 1800–1923* (Madison: University of Wisconsin Press, 1982), 8.

61. Max Weinreich, "YIVO and the Problems of our Time," *Yivobleter* 25, no. 1 (1945), 13.

62. J. L. Talmon, *Israel Among the Nations* (London: Weindenfeld & Nicolson, 1970), 9.

63. Elon, *Jewish Law*, 64–74

64. Gerald J. Blidstein, "The State and the Legitimate Use of Force and Coercion in Modern Halakhic Thought," in *Jews and Violence: Images, Ideologies, Realities*, ed. Peter Y. Medding, *Studies in Contemporary Jewry* XVIII (New York: Oxford University Press, 2002), 5.

65. Here I am paraphrasing the helpful formulation of Eli Lederhendler in *The Road to Modern Jewish Politics: Political Tradition and Political Reconstruction in the Jewish Community of Tsarist Russia* (New York: Oxford University Press, 1989), 33–34.

66. Esther 3:8–11, in *Tanakh*, 1460–61.

67. Yoram Hazony, *The Dawn: Political Teachings of the Book of Esther* (Jerusalem: Genesis Jerusalem Press, 1995), 4.

68. Yosef Kaplan, "Court Jews Before the Hofjuden," in *From Court Jews to the Rothschilds*, ed. Vivian B. Mann and Richard I. Cohen (Munich: Jewish Museum and Prestel-Verlag, 1996), 13.

69. Excerpts from the statute in Eli Barnavi, *A Historical Atlas of the Jewish People from the Time of the Patriarchs to the Present* (New York: Schocken, 1992), 119.

70. Gershon Hundert, *Jews in Poland-Lithuania in the Eighteenth Century* (Berkeley: University of California Press, 2004), 12–13, passim.

71. Chone Shmeruk, *The Esterke Story in Yiddish and Polish Literature: A*

Case Study in the Mutual Relations of Two Cultural Traditions (Jerusalem: Zalman Shazar Center, 1985).

72. Shlomo Dov Goitein, "Political Conflict and the Use of Power in the World of the Geniza," in Elazar, *Kinship and Consent*, 177.

73. Gerson D. Cohen, "Changing Perspectives of Jewish Historiography," in *Jewish History and Jewish Destiny*, foreword by Neil Gillman (New York: Jewish Theological Seminary, 1997), 172.

74. For discussion of the middleman theory as it applies to the Jews, see Walter P. Zenner, "The Jewish Diaspora and the Middleman Adaptation," in *Diaspora: Exile and the Jewish Condition*, ed. Etan Levine (New York: Jason Aronson, 1983), 141–56.

75. Thomas Sowell, "Are Jews Generic?" in *Black Rednecks and White Liberals* (San Francisco: Encounter Books, 2005), 69ff.

76. Simon Ravidowicz coined the phrase "ever-dying people" in the title essay *Israel, the Ever-Dying People and other Essays*, ed. Benjamin C. I. Ravid (Rutherford, N.J.: Fairleigh Dickinson University Press), 1986.

77. Yizhak F. Baer, *Galut* (Exile), trans. Robert Warshow (New York: Schocken Books, 1947), 110.

78. Saul Tchernikhovsky, *"Shalosh atonot"* (Three Donkeys, dated June 7, 1939) in *Shirim* (Collected Poems), vol. 1 (Tel Aviv: Dvir, 1966), 460.

79. "The battle of Khyber was a turning point in the defeat of the Jews of the Province of Hejaz and a victory for Islam." This is the summary of Islam's relation to the Jews on the al-islam.org Web site.

80. Paul Johnson, *A History of the Jews* (New York: Harper & Row, 1987), 164.

81. See, e.g., Yitzhak Baer, *A History of the Jews in Christian Spain*, vol. 1, trans. Louis Schoffman (Philadelphia: Jewish Publication Society, 1961), 138–50.

82. Hyam Maccoby, *Judaism on Trial: Jewish-Christian Disputations in the Middle Ages* (Rutherford, N.J.: Fairleigh Dickinson University Press, 1982), 39.

83. Robert Chazan, *Barcelona and Beyond: The Disputation of 1263 and its Aftermath* (Berkeley: University of California Press, 1992), 51.

84. Maccoby, 105ff.

85. Ibid., 109 and footnote.

86. Ibid., 119–20.

87. Paul Johnson sums up this episode with verve and clarity in his *History of the Jews*, 219.

88. Maccoby, 149. Maccoby's translation from the Latin is based on the Christian account of the disputation.

89. Chazan, 196.

90. This argument is indebted to Haim Beinart, "The Conversos and Their Fate," in *Spain and the Jews: The Sephardi Experience 1491 and After*, ed. Elie Kedouri (London: Thames and Hudson, 1992), 92–122, and Baer, *A History of the Jews in Christian Spain*, vol. 2 (Philadelphia: Jewish Publication Society, 1961), 244–99.

91. See Emanuel Quint, *A Restatement of Rabbinic Civil Law*, vol. 10 (Jerusalem: Gefen, 2004), 65–77.

92. Yehushua Hana Ravnitsky, *Yidishe vitsn* (Jewish Jokes) (Berlin: Moriah, 1923), 57.

93. The political principle governing such action was articulated by the chief rabbi of Moscow, Ya'akov Mazeh, who in 1920 asked Leon Trotsky (born Lev Bronstein), head of the Red Army, to use his power to protect the Jews from pogromist attacks. When Trotsky declined to intervene on the grounds that he was not a Jew, Rabbi Mazeh said, "That's the tragedy. It's the Trotskys who make revolutions, and the Bronsteins who pay the price."

94. David G. Roskies, *The Literature of Destruction: Jewish Responses to Catastrophe* (Philadelphia: Jewish Publication Society, 1989).

95. H[alper] Leivick, *Complete Works by H. Leivick* (in Yiddish) (New York: Shoulson, 1940), vol. I, 648.

Part Two

1. Berr Isaac Berr, "Lettre d'un Citoyen" (Nancy, 1791), reprinted from M. Diogene Tama, *Transactions of the Parisian Sanhedrin*, trans. F. D. Kirwan (London 1807), in *The Jew in the Modern World*, ed. Paul Mendes-Flohr and Jehuda Reinharz (New York: Oxford University Press, 1980), 107–8.

2. Ibid., 104, 108.

3. Stefan Zweig, *The World of Yesterday* (1943; repr., Lincoln, Neb.: University of Nebraska Press, 1964), 22.

4. Howard Sachar, *A History of the Jews in the Modern World* (New York: Alfred A. Knopf, 2005), 85.

5. Heinrich Graetz, *History of the Jews*, vol. 5, ed. and in part trans. Bella Lowy (Philadelphia: Jewish Publication Society, 1945), 632–33.

6. Simon Dubnow, *History of the Jews*, vol. 5, trans. Moshe Spiegel (South Brunswick, N.J.: Thomas Yoseloff, 1973), 250–51.

7. Sachar, *A History of the Jews in the Modern World*, 85.

8. This interpretation of the case owes much to Jonathan Frankel's exemplary study *The Damascus Affair: "Ritual Murder," Politics, and the Jews in 1840* (Cambridge, England: Cambridge University Press, 1997). See especially pp. 437–41.

9. Ibid., 441.

10. Jacob Katz, *From Prejudice to Destruction: Anti-Semitism, 1700–1933* (Cambridge, Mass.: Harvard University Press, 1980), 3.

11. G. E. Lessing, *The Jews*, in *The German-Jewish Dialogue: An Anthology of Literary Texts, 1749–1993*, ed. Ritchie Robertson (Oxford, England: Oxford University Press, 1999), 13.

12. Wilhelm Marr, "The Victory of Jewry over Germandom" (1879), in *Antisemitism in the Modern World: An Anthology of Texts*, ed. Richard S. Levy (Lexington, Mass.: D. C. Heath and Company, 1991), 80.

13. Ibid., 79.

14. Ibid., 83.

15. Thinkers much more sophisticated than Marr likewise identified features of Jewish self-adaptation as the cause of European decline. "Where Luther and Fichte had denounced the Jews as aliens who robbed the German peasant of his patrimony, Oswald Spengler and the Blut und Boden [Blood and Soil] school argued that the Jewish nature was incapable of striking root in any soil and was the carrier of decadence; only those with ancient ties to the land they inhabited could nourish a living culture. Judaism had become the plague of the west, and the spread of its influence a symptom of the disintegration of the European world. Judaism's cosmopolitanism was contagious, destructive of all

values: this was the obverse of the Jewish exclusiveness condemned in antiquity. Judaism shaped a Levantine personality that could assimilate all cultures but could create nothing of its own. Judaism was equivalent to parasitism—a later mainstay of Nazi propaganda." Frank E. Manuel, *The Broken Staff: Judaism Through Christian Eyes* (Cambridge, Mass.: Harvard University Press, 1992), 295.

16. Moshe Zimmermann has provided a careful and unusually empathetic study of the man and the process in *Wilhelm Marr: The Patriarch of Anti-Semitism* (New York: Oxford University Press, 1986), 89–95.

17. Norman Cohn, *Warrant for Genocide: The Myth of the Jewish World Conspiracy and the Protocols of the Elders of Zion* (London: Serif, 1996), 28–29.

18. Paul Berman, *Terror and Liberalism* (New York: W. W. Norton & Co., 2003), 42.

19. Lueger won his first election in 1895, but Emperor Franz Joseph did not allow him to assume the office until his third election in 1897. He served until 1910.

20. Stefan Zweig, who presents Lueger as the prototype for Adolf Hitler, nevertheless recalls the gentleness and "democratic justice" of his administration as compared with the destruction to come. See his *The World of Yesterday*, 62.

21. Benjamin W. Segal, *The Greatest Lie in History: The Protocols of the Elders of Zion*, trans. Sascha Czaczkes-Charles (New York: Bloch, 1934), 7. When his book exposing this forgery was originally published in Germany in 1924, Segal urged its dissemination as a necessary antidote to the force he foresaw might bring Hitler to power.

22. Anonymous, *Protocols of the Learned Elders of Zion*, trans. Victor E. Marsden (Los Angeles: Christian Nationalist Crusade, no date), 11. This is Protocol 1, point 6.

23. See Ibid, Protocol 18.

24. Karl Marx, "On the Jewish Question," in *Early Writings*, trans. and ed. T. B. Bottomore, foreword by Erich Fromm (New York: McGraw Hill, 1963), 3–40. See also Julius Carlebach, *Karl Marx and the Radical Critique of Judaism* (London: Routledge and Kegan Paul, 1978), especially pp. 148–84.

25. Robert S. Wistrich, *Antisemitism: The Longest Hatred* (New York: Pantheon Books, 1991). See also the documentary based on this book, directed Rex Bloomstein, 1993. Israel Zangwill's formulation "The law of dislike for the unlike will always prevail" was used by Salo Baron during his testimony at the Eichmann trial to define anti-Semitism.

Part Three

1. S. Y. Agnon, *Only Yesterday*, trans. Barbara Harshav (Princeton: Princeton University Press, 2000), 39.

2. Historians have recently developed an interest in movements of ascent (*aliyah*) to the Land of Israel from the time of the Crusades until the nineteenth century. "Some of these aliyot were unknown to us until recently; in other cases, recent research has added substantial detail to the historical record. . . . Although the number of Jews who succeeded in making the voyage and settling in Palestine never constituted more than a small portion of world Jewry, these messianic aliyot were of enduring significance, partly because of the renown of those who took part, partly because of their regular appearance over the centuries, and partly because of the variety of diaspora communities which participated. The messianic impulse which spawned these waves of immigration, and the belief in the centrality of the land of Israel upon which they depended, were in no way marginal to the Jewish tradition, but in fact became an axis of Jewish spiritual life." See Arie Morgenstern, "Dispersion and the Longing for Zion," *Azure* (Winter 2002), 75–76.

3. Judah Halevi, *"Libi bemizrakh,"* in *The Penguin Book of Hebrew Verse*, ed. Ted Carmi (New York: Viking and The Jewish Publication Society, 1981), 347.

4. Heinrich Heine, "Jehuda Ben Halevy," trans. Aaron Kramer, in *The Poetry and Prose of Heinrich Heine*, ed. Frederic Ewen (New York: Citadel Press, 1948), 288.

5. Ibid., 289.

6. "I have left behind all my loved ones, I have quit my native home. I've abandoned myself to the sea: Carry me, Sea, to mother's bosom!

And you loyal West Wind, drive my ship to that shore, whither my heart on eagle's wings has long been seeking a path." Yehuda Halevi, *"Kh'hob farlozn mayne libste,"* trans. Chaim Nahman Bialik, music by M. Shneyer, published by Jos. P. Katz, New York, in 1917. In *Pearls of Yiddish Song*, ed. Eleanor Gordon Mlotek and Joseph Mlotek (New York: Workmen's Circle, 1988), 212–13.

7. Moses Hess, *The Revival of Israel: Rome and Jerusalem, the Last Nationalist Question*, trans. Meyer Waxman (Lincoln, Neb.: University of Nebraska Press, 1995), 74.

8. Ben-Zion Dinur, *Israel and the Diaspora*, trans. Merton B. Dagut (Philadelphia: Jewish Publication Society, 1969), 141, 145.

9. See Hannah Arendt's development of this thesis in *The Origins of Totalitaranism* (Cleveland, Ohio: World Publishing Co., 1958), part one, 3–53.

10. Moshe Leib Lilienblum, "The Future of Our People" (1883), *The Zionist Idea*, trans. and ed. Arthur Hertzberg (New York: Atheneum, 1971), 175.

11. M. L. (Moshe Leib) Lilienblum, editorial, *Der yiddisher veker* (The Jewish Awakener), Odessa, 1887.

12. See Ernst Pawel, *The Labyrinth of Exile* (New York: Farrar, Straus and Giroux, 1989), chap. 12; Theodor Herzl, *The Jewish State: An Attempt at a Modern Solution of the Jewish Question*, trans. Sylvie D'Avigdor, revised with foreword by Israel Cohen (London: H. Pordes, 1972), 7.

13. Ella Florsheim, "Giving Herzl His Due," *Azure* 21 (Summer 2005), 20.

14. Herzl, *The Jewish State*, 71–75.

15. Ibid., 79.

16. The prominent Polish liberal Aleksander Swietochowski claimed that salt can dissolve in water only in modest quantities, but too much Jewish salt was proving indissoluble.

17. Theodor Herzl, *Old-New Land*, trans. Lotta Levensohn, preface by Stephen S. Wise (New York: Bloch Publishing Co., 1941), 66.

18. Theodor Herzl, *Altneuland* (Vienna: Hans Deutsch Verlag, 1962),

53. *"Wir fragen nicht, welchen Glaubens und welcher Rasse einer ist. Ein Mensch soll er sein, das genugt uns."*

19. Herzl, *Old-New Land*, 259.

20. Ibid., 76.

21. Ibid., 76–77.

22. Ibid., 123–24.

23. Steven J. Zipperstein, *Elusive Prophet: Ahad Ha'am and the Origins of Zionism* (Berkeley: University of California, 1993), 196. Zipperstein gives a lively account of the feud in Zionist ranks over this novel.

24. Ahad Ha'am (Asher Ginsberg), "The Jewish State and the Jewish Problem," trans. Arthur Herzberg in *The Zionist Idea*, 268. See, e.g., Jacques Kornberg, "Ahad Ha-am and Herzl" in his edition of essays on Ahad Ha'am, *At the Crossroads* (Albany: SUNY Press, 1983), 106–29.

25. Ahad Ha'am, introduction to the first edition, *Kal Kitvei Ahad Ha'am* (Collected Writings, Tel Aviv and Jerusalem: Dvir and Hotza'a Ivrit, 1959), 3. As quoted by Gideon Shimoni, *The Zionist Ideology* (Hanover, N.H.: Brandeis University Press, 1995), III.

26. Herzl, *Old-New Land*, 91–92.

27. George Eliot, *Daniel Deronda*, ed. Graham Handley (Oxford, England: Oxford University Press, 1988), 688.

28. This view of Grandcourt owes much to Irving Howe, "George Eliot and Radical Evil," in his *Selected Writings, 1950–1990* (San Diego: Harcourt Brace Jovanovich, 1990), 347–362.

29. Letter, dated Feb. 6, 1883, to E. R. A. Seligman, in ed. Bette Roth Young, *Emma Lazarus in Her World: Life and Letters* (Philadelphia: Jewish Publication Society, 1995) 202–3.

30. Israel Zangwill, "Samooborona," in the collection *Ghetto Comedies* (New York: Macmillan, 1907), 483.

31. Ezra Mendelsohn, *Modern Jewish Politics* (New York: Oxford University Press, 1992), 3.

32. For a basic description of the five, see www.zionism-israel.com/dic/Aliyot.htm.

33. Dvorah Dayan, "My Aliyah to the Land of Israel," in *The Plough Woman: Records of the Pioneer Women of Palestine*, ed. Mark A. Raider and

Miriam B. Raider-Roth (Hanover, N.H.: Brandeis University Press, 2002), 35, 36.

34. Moshe Dayan, *Story of My Life: An Autobiography* (New York: William Morrow, 1976), 82.

35. Yaacov Shimoni, ed., *Political Dictionary of the Arab World* (New York: Macmillan, 1987), 80. The non-Arab or semi-Arab countries, Mauritania, Somalia, and Djibouti, joined subsequently.

36. Minutes of the Fourth Conference of Ahdut ha-Avoda, Tel Aviv, 1926, p. 35. Quoted by Anita Shapira, *Berl: The Biography of a Socialist Zionist* (Cambridge, England: Cambridge University Press, 1980), 167.

37. Ben Halpern and Jehuda Reinharz, *Zionism and the Creation of a New Society* (Hanover, N.H.: Brandeis University Press, 2000), 241.

38. S. An-sky, "The Destruction of Galicia," trans. Golda Werman, in David G. Roskies, ed. *The Dybbuk and Other Writings* (New Haven, Conn.: Yale University Press, 2002), 172.

39. See Martin Sugarman, "The Zion Muleteers of Gallipoli (March 1915–May 1916)," Jewishvirtuallibrary.org/jsource/history/gallipoli/html.

40. Shmuel Katz, *Lone Wolf: A Biography of Vladimir Ze'ev Jabotinsky*, vol. 1 (New York: Barricade Books, 1996), 156.

41. Ze'ev Jabotinsky, *Autobiography*, quoted in ibid., I, 148.

42. Article 2 of the Mandate for Palestine.

43. Sachar, *A History of the Jews in the Modern World*, 572.

44. Arthur Koestler, *Thieves in the Night* (London: Macmillan, 1946). See also David Cesarani, *Arthur Koestler: The Homeless Mind* (London: William Heinemann, 1998), 246.

45. Letter to Menahem Ussishkin, November 11, 1936, quoted in Nathan Yanai, "Ben-Gurion's Concept of *Mamlahtiut* and the Forming Reality of the State of Israel," *Jewish Political Studies Review*, vol. 1, nos. 1–2 (Spring 1989), 154–55.

46. Eric Silver: *Begin: The Haunted Prophet* (New York: Random House, 1984), 98ff.

47. Koestler, *Thieves in the Night*, 295.

48. Shabtai Teveth, *Ben-Gurion: The Burning Ground, 1886–1948* (Boston: Houghton Mifflin Co., 1987), 460–461. See the fuller story in

Teveth, *Ben-Gurion and the Palestinian Arabs: From Peace to War* (Oxford, England: Oxford University Press, 1985).

49. Shimoni, *Political Dictionary of the Arab World*, 217.

50. See, inter alia, Daniel Carpi, "The Mufti of Jerusalem, Amin el-Husseini, and His Diplomatic Activity During World War II," *Studies in Zionism* 7 (Spring 1983), 101–131; and D. Carpi, "The Diplomatic Negotiations over the Transfer of Jewish Children from Croatia to Turkey and Palestine in 1943," *Yad Vashem Studies* 12 (1977), 109–24.

51. Speech by Ridwan al Hilw, Palestinian delegate at the Seventh Congress of the Comintern, Free Arab Voice, July 31, 1935. Trans. from the French by Kevin Walsh. www.freearabvoice.org.

52. These are phrases from the preamble to the Charter of the United Nations.

53. The Arab League Charter, March 22, 1945, undertakes to appoint a representative on behalf of Palestine.

54. Hossein Shariatmadari, editor of the *Kayhan* daily. As reported by MSNBC, October 30, 2005.

55. *Near East Report*, December 16, 2002.

56. Mitchell Bard, "The Arab Boycott," Web site of Jewish Virtual Library of the American-Israeli Cooperative Enterprise.

57. Cairo Radio, July 19, 1957, as quoted by Paul Johnson, *A History of the Jews* (New York: Harper and Row, 1987), 530.

58. Signe Gilen, Are Hovdenak, et al., *Finding Ways: Palestinian Coping Strategies in Changing Environments* (Norway: FAFO, 1994), 21.

59. Israel High Tech and Investment Report of June 2005.

60. As reported by Norman Podhoretz, "The State of World Jewry," *Commentary* (December 1983), 39.

61. A nuanced history of this crisis and its aftermath is Michael B. Oren, *Six Days of War: June 1967 and the Making of the Modern Middle East* (Oxford, England: Oxford University Press, 2002).

62. There was no issue, writes Anita Shapira in her authoritative study of Israel's relation to power,

in which the lack of symmetry in respect to Jewish-Arab relations was so pronounced as the issue of self-restraint. In Arab eyes, every Jew, by dint of being a Jew, was regarded as an enemy; right from the outset, the struggle had been viewed as total. From the Jewish perspective, an intellectual, psychological, and political effort was made to maintain a differentiated image of the Arab. It is thus not surprising that while terrorists were praised on the Arab side as national heroes, and no moderates spoke out against acts of murder and brutality, similar outrages by the Jewish side met with shock and profound misgivings among the Jews.

Anita Shapira, *Land and Power: The Zionist Resort to Force 1881–1948* (New York: Oxford University Press, 1992), 236.

63. Mohamed Hassanein Heikal, in *Al-Ahram*, March 7, 1969. Cited in Yaacov Bar-Siman-Tov, *The Israeli-Egyptian War of Attrition 1969–1970* (New York: Columbia University Press, 1980), 55.

64. British Foreign Office File 371/20822E7201/22/31. The text appears with commentary in Elie Kedouri, *Islam and the Modern World and Other Studies* (London: Mansell, 1980), 72. Cited by Robert Wistrich, *Antisemitism, The Longest Hatred* (London: Thames Methuen, 1991), 233.

65. Friday sermon on PA TV, delivered by Dr. Mahmoud Mustafah Najem in the Sheikh Ejlin Mosque in Gaza, broadcast on Palestinian Authority TV, November 1, 2002, posted by Itamar Marcus, Palestinian Media Watch, November 4, 2002. Videos of similar sermons can be found at www.pmw.org.il/tv%20part6.html and through MEMRI postings.

66. Meron Benvenisti, *Conflicts and Contradictions* (New York: Villard, 1986), 70. Quoted by Edward Alexander in his essay "Israelis Against Themselves," in *The Jewish Divide over Israel*, ed. Edward Alexander and Paul Bogdanor (New Brunswick, N.J.: Transaction Publishers, 2006), 33–45.

67. Amos Oz, "The Hamas-Likud Connection," *New York Times*, April 11, 1995.

68. Jonathan Tobin, "Who Really Teaches Hatred?" in *Jewish World Review*, July 27, 2006.

69. "Sadat's 'Sacred' Mission," *Time Europe*, November 28, 1977.

70. Tamar Liebes, "Falling in Love with the Enemy: Sadat's Visit to Jerusalem as a Media Event," speech delivered at a Hebrew University

seminar commemorating the twenty-fifth anniversary of the visit, November 26, 2002.

71. Ezer Weizman, *The Battle for Peace* (Toronto: Bantam Books, 1981), 122–25. At one point, writes Weizman, they felt "like guests at someone else's wedding."

72. Anwar Sadat, address to the Israeli Knesset, November 20, 1977.

73. This was pointed out by the Jewish educator Ephraim Buchwald.

74. Mahmoud Abbas, *"Al-Wajh al-ākhar: Al-alāqāt al-sirrīyah bayna al-Nāzīyah wa-al-Ṣihyūnīyah"* (The Other Side: The Secret Relations Between Nazism and the Leadership of the Zionist Movement) Friendship University, (Moscow, 1983), trans. Simon Wiesenthal Center.

75. Anis Al-Qasim, *Min Al-Tih ilal-Quds* (From the Wilderness to Jerusalem) (Tripoli, Libya: 1965), 17. Quoted by Yehoshafat Harkabi, "The Palestinians in the Fifties and Their Awakening as Reflected in Their Literature," in *Palestinian Arab Politics*, ed. Moshe Ma'oz (Jerusalem: Jerusalem Academic Press, 1975), 53.

76. Rashid Khalidi, *Palestinian Identity: The Construction of Modern National Consciousness* (New York: Columbia University Press, 1997), 11.

77. These examples are drawn from www.Jerusalemites.org; alnakba.org; and the Web site of the Khalil Sakakini Cultural Center. The Muslim Council of Britain (representing 350 organizations) annually announces its refusal to attend Holocaust Memorial Day on the grounds that the ceremonies ignore ongoing genocide in the "Occupied Territories of Palestine" and because it "should include al nakba."

78. www.palestinecalendar.org.

79. Jean-Paul Sartre, *Anti-Semite and Jew* (*Reflexions sur la question juive*), trans. George J. Becker (New York: Grove Press, 1948), 13.

80. Leo Strauss, "Why We Remain Jews," in *Jewish Philosophy and the Crisis of Modernity: Essays and Lectures in Modern Jewish Thought*, ed. Kenneth Hart Green (Albany: SUNY Press, 1997), 321.

81. Abu Salma (Abd al-Kareem al-Karmi), "We Shall Return," trans. Sharif Elmusa and Naomi Shihab Nye, in *Anthology of Modern Palestinian Literature*, ed. Salma Khadra Jayyusi (New York: Columbia University Press, 1992), 96.

82. Ibid., 97.

83. Rashid Husain, "Against," trans. May Jayyusi and Naomi Shihab Nye, in Jayyusi, *Anthology of Modern Palestinian Literature*, 175.

84. Thomas Friedman, "Promised Land: Israel and the Palestinians See a Way to Co-Exist," New York Times, Sept. 5, 1993.

85. Quoted in *Yediot Aharonot*, September 3, 1993, cited by Ze'ev Binyamin Begin, "Rabin's Self-Entrapment," *Jerusalem Post*, September 9, 1993.

86. Yossi Beilin, *Touching Peace: From the Oslo Accord to a Final Agreement*, trans. Philip Simpson (London: Weidenfeld & Nicolson, 1999); Mahmud Abbas, *Through Secret Channels* (Reading, England: Garnet. 1995); Uri Savir, *The Process: 1,000 Days That Changed the Middle East* (New York: Random House, 1998).

87. Ziyad Abu 'Ein, interview on Al-Alam TV, July 4, 2006, trans. Middle East Media Research Institute.

88. Nadav Shragai, "We Deserve the Qassams and the Katyushas," *Ha'aretz*, July 16, 2006.

89. Norman Podhoretz, "America and Israel: An Ominous Change," *Commentary* (January 1992), 23.

90. Jean-François Revel, *How Democracies Perish*, with the assistance of Branko Lazitch, trans. William Byron (New York: Harper & Row, 1983), 3

91. Ibid., 4–5.

92. Wyndham Lewis, *The Jews: Are They Human?* (London: George Allen and Unwin, 1939), 109.

93. Bernard Lewis: *What Went Wrong? Western Impact and Middle Eastern Response* (New York: Oxford University Press, 2002).

94. David Biale, *Power and Powerlessness in Jewish History* (New York: Schocken Books, 1986), 5.

95. Ibid., 21–22.

96. An-sky (Rappoport), "The Jewish Folk-Spirit and What It Wrought," in *Gezamlte Shriftn* (Collected Works, vol. 15, Vilna: Shreberk, 1923), 23–24.

97. Conor Cruise O'Brien, *The Siege: The Saga of Israel and Zionism* (New York: Simon and Schuster, 1986).

98. Mitchell J. Cohen, *Churchill and the Jews*, 2nd. rev. ed. (London: Frank Cass, 1985), 287.

99. Michael Beschloss, *The Conquerors: Roosevelt, Truman, and the Destruction of Hitler's Germany 1941–1945* (New York: Simon and Schuster, 2002), 41. Here, as in the case of Churchill, apologists and detractors argue over a record that—when all is said and done—plainly left the European Jews to their fate.

100. Patrick J. Buchanan, "Whose War?" *American Conservative*, March 24, 2003.

101. James Woolsey, "We Are All Jews Now," *Jerusalem Post*, September 26, 2003.

102. Pierre Van Paassen, *The Forgotten Ally* (New York: Dial Press, 1943).

103. Sebastian Haffner, *Defying Hitler: A Memoir*, trans. Oliver Pretzel (New York: Farrar, Straus and Giroux, 2002), 142.

104. Anne Bayefsky, "Had Enough?" from *National Review Online*, July 17, 2004. Based on her longer analyses, including "Israel and the United Nations' Human Rights Agenda: The Inequality of Nations Large and Small," *Israel Law Review* 29, no. 3 (1995). See testimony of Ambassador Morris B. Abram in "The Treatment of Israel by the United Nations," read before the House Committee on International Relations, July 14, 1999.

CHRONOLOGY

c. 1250 BCE   The Israelites, led by Joshua, conquer the Land of Israel.

c. 1000-922 BCE   King David and his son King Solomon rule a united Jewish kingdom in the Land of Israel.

721 BCE   The ten northern tribes of Israel are defeated by the Assyrians and taken into exile.

586 BCE   The kingdom of Judah is defeated by the Babylonians and its leaders exiled to Babylon.

539 BCE   The Persian emperor Cyrus the Great, having defeated the Babylonian Empire, allows exiled Jews to begin to return to the Land of Israel and to rebuild the Temple.

458 BCE   Another community of exiled Jews, led by Ezra, returns to the Land of Israel.

410 BCE   Anti-Jewish riots lead to the destruction of the Jewish temple at Elephantine, Egypt;

it is rebuilt with Persian authorization in 400 BCE.

332 BCE   Alexander the Great conquers the Land of Israel.

c. 300–250 BCE   Emergence of Septuagint, the Greek translation of the Bible, composed for the benefit of Greek-speaking Jews in Alexandria.

167 BCE   The Maccabees launch an ultimately successful revolt against the hellenizing ruler Antiochus IV Epiphanes.

37–4 BCE   Herod ("the Great") ruled as king over Judea after his appointment by Rome. Famous for horrific brutality against political opponents and rivals, he is also a successful military and political leader and initiates massive building and reconstruction projects, including the Temple in Jerusalem.

38 CE   Riots against the Jews of Alexandria.

70   The emperor Titus crushes the Jewish revolt against Roman rule, burning the Temple in Jerusalem and sending many Jews into exile. Rabbinic academy is established in the city of Yavneh in northern Israel.

115–17 Revolt of Jews in Cyrene, Egypt, and Cyprus.

135 Romans brutally defeat the second Jewish revolt in the Land of Israel, led by Bar Kokhba.

c. 200 The Mishnah, a collection of Rabbinic laws derived from the Torah, is codified.

312 The Roman emperor Constantine begins to favor the Christian church; restrictions on Jews in the Roman Empire follow later in the fourth century, placing them in a position secondary to Christians and making their proselytizing illegal.

622 Muhammad and his followers emigrate to Medina from Mecca; the beginning of the Muslim era.

1038 Shmuel Ha-Nagid becomes vizier of Muslim Granada.

1066 First persecution of Jews in Muslim Spain takes place in Granada.

1096 Crusaders massacre Jews across France, the Rhineland, and Bohemia on their way to Jerusalem; Jews attempt to pay the Christian rulers of their cities for protection.

1144 First blood libel takes place in Norwich, England.

1146 The Second Crusade marches across Europe to Israel; Jewish communities are attacked, but the attacks are much less severe than those of the First Crusade.

1190 King Richard I brings the crusading spirit to England; Jews are massacred around the country.

1239 King James I invites Jews to settle in Barcelona, and grants the Jewish religious courts authority over disputes between Jews.

1263 The Disputation of Barcelona, in which Nachmanides, a rabbi, and Pablo Christiani, a Jewish apostate, debate the theological veracity of their traditions.

1264 Duke Boleslaw of Poland issues proclamation granting Jews generous legal and political rights. His successor, King Casimir, further extends the favorable treatment of Jews.

1290 The Jews are expelled from England by King Edward I.

1394 Expulsion of the Jews from France.

1453 The Ottomans conquer Constantinople, invite Jews to return to the city.

1492 King Ferdinand and Queen Isabella, having united Spain under Christian rule, compel the Jews to leave Spain or convert to Christianity; those that stay are subject to the Inquisition, and many are executed as false converts.

1497 Expulsion of the Jews from Portugal.

1516 The Ottomans defeat the Mamelukes, beginning four
hundred years of Ottoman rule of the Land of Israel.

1580 Establishment in Lublin, Poland, of the Council of
the Four Lands (Greater Poland, Little Poland,
Ruthenia, and Volhynia), an autonomous governing
body overseeing taxation and charitable and
communal institutions and ruling on religious and
often civil matters according to Jewish law.

1648 Peasant uprising in Ukraine led by Bogdan
Chmielnicki destroys hundreds of Jewish
communities.

1654 Arrival of first Jews in New World, from Recife to
New Amsterdam.

1655 Under Cromwell, Jews are permitted to return to
England.

1764 The Polish government disestablishes the Council of
the Four Lands.

1789 Establishment of the United States of America as a
democracy open to members of all religious groups.

1791 Emancipation of the Jews of France.

1796 Emancipation of the Jews of the Netherlands.

1818 The first Reform synagogue opens in Hamburg;

its services include prayer in the vernacular, a more decorous style influenced by Christian worship, and fewer references to the return to Zion.

1840 The Damascus Affair, in which prominent Syrian Jews are accused of the ritual murder of an Italian monk in Damascus; Jews from western Europe eventually intervene and save the lives of several of the accused.

1848 Spain declares equal political and civil rights for all citizens, regardless of religion.

1858 Emancipation of the Jews of England.

1860 Alliance Israelite Universelle, the first international Jewish organization, is founded in Paris to protect Jews around the world who suffer from discrimination.

1867 Full civil rights are granted to Jews in Austria-Hungary.

1871 Consolidation of the German Reich and abolition of restrictions on the political and civil rights of Jews and other religious minorities.

1876 George Eliot publishes *Daniel Deronda*, a novel that encourages Jews to realize their own national aspirations.

1879 Wilhelm Marr publishes "The Victory of Jewry over Germandom," in which he coins the term "anti-Semitism."

1881   In response to a wave of pogroms in Russia, Leo
        Pinsker calls for Jewish self-emancipation.

1882   Members of Hibbat Tziyon (the Lovers of Zion)
        begin to immigrate to Israel in a movement that will
        become known as the First Aliyah.

1886   First publication of the poem "Hatikvah," by
        Naphtali Herz Imber, which would become Israel's
        national anthem.

        Publication of Édouard Drumont's anti-Semitic *La
        France Juive.*

1889   Ahad Ha'am, a leading Zionist thinker, begins
        publishing essays that helped shape a modern Jewish
        philosophy of identity.

1894   Captain Alfred Dreyfus framed for treason to France,
        convicted and sentenced to life imprisonment amid
        tremendous wave of anti-Semitic sentiment in France.

1897   Theodor Herzl holds a Zionist Congress in Basel;
        within one year, the emerging Zionist movement has
        eight hundred chapters across Europe, representing
        more than 100,000 Jews.

        Karl Lueger wins election as mayor of Vienna on anti-
        Semitic platform.

1901   The Fifth Zionist Congress establishes the Jewish
        National Fund, to purchase and develop land in Israel.

1902 Herzl publishes *Altneuland* (*Old-New Land*), his utopian vision of a liberal Jewish state in the Land of Israel.

1904–14 The Second Aliyah, a wave of immigration, brings 40,000 Jews, most of them from Russia, to the Land of Israel.

1905 The first publication, in Russia, of the anti-Semitic forgery *Protocols of the Elders of Zion*.

1909 Hashomer, a small guild of watchmen to guard Jewish settlements in Palestine, is founded.

1910 Eliezer Ben Yehuda, the great reviver of modern Hebrew, begins to publish his *Complete Dictionary of Ancient and Modern Hebrew*.

1912 Founding of Tel Aviv, the first modern Jewish city in the land of Israel, named after the Hebrew title of Herzl's *Altneuland*.

Joseph Trumpeldor, a Russian war hero and the first Jew to be granted officer's rank under the czar, immigrates to Palestine; he is expelled by the Turks after the outbreak of World War I and then fights for the British.

1917 Ze'ev Jabotinsky organizes the Jewish Legion as part of the British army in World War I; he hopes it will eventually become a Jewish army that will defend the Land of Israel.

British conquer the Land of Israel from the Ottoman Empire.

November 2, 1917 The British government issues the Balfour Declaration, promising "the establishment in Palestine of a national home for the Jewish people."

1918 Chaim Weizmann founds the Hebrew University in Jerusalem; Albert Einstein and other prominent Jewish intellectuals help with fund-raising for the university, which opens in 1923.

1920 Haj Amin el-Husseini pioneers anti-Jewish terror in an attack at the Western Wall in Jerusalem.

December 1920 The Trade Union Movement (Histadrut) sets up a national defense organization— Haganah—"to safeguard the national and social content of popular defense" in the Land of Israel.

1921 Sir Herbert Samuel, British high commissioner in Palestine, appoints Husseini Grand Mufti of Jerusalem.

1922 Iraq and Egypt win independence from British rule; Britain establishes the Emirate of Transjordan.

1925   First meeting of the Union of Zionists-
Revisionists in Paris; influenced by
Jabotinsky, the Revisionists insist that
gaining political autonomy is central to the
Zionist project and are willing to use arms
to achieve it.

1929   Arab riots in Hebron and Safed, organized by
the Grand Mufti of Jerusalem.

1930   Founding of Mapai, the political party born
of the union of the Ahdut ha-Avodah and
Ha-Po'el ha-Za'ir parties; this Zionist-
Socialist party became the dominant party
in the *yishuv*, the pre-state Jewish authority
in the Land of Israel, and remained dominant
through the first decades of the state
of Israel.

1931   The Irgun, an independent Jewish militia,
is founded under the leadership of Ze'ev
Jabotinsky of the Revisionist party.

January 1933   Adolf Hitler is appointed chancellor of
Germany.

1934   Russia, under Stalin, establishes "Jewish
autonomous region" in Birobidzhan;
encourages Jews to settle in this officially
Yiddish-speaking area.

September 1935   Hitler declares the Nuremberg Race Laws, depriving German Jews of their citizenship.

1936–37   Husseini organizes the "Great Revolt" against British.

March 1938   Nazi troops enter Austria; Hitler announces that Austria is now united with Germany.

October 1938   Neville Chamberlain, prime minister of Great Britain, signs the Munich agreement, which grants Germany the Sudetenland; Chamberlain assures the world he has brought "peace in our time."

November 9, 1938   Following the murder of a German diplomat in Paris by a Jew whose parents had been deported from Germany, Jews throughout Germany are attacked in a massive, coordinated wave of violence known as *Kristallnacht*, or Night of Broken Glass.

1939   British White Paper limits Jewish immigration to Palestine to 75,000 over the next five years.

September 1939   Germany invades Poland; Britain and France declare war on Germany.

Chronology

December 1941	Japan attacks the United States at Pearl Harbor; United States enters the war against Japan and Germany.
1942	The jurist Raphael Lemkin coins term "genocide" to describe the extermination of an entire people.
January 1942	First mass gassings of Jews at Auschwitz.
May 7, 1945	Germany unconditionally surrenders to the Allies.
November 29, 1947	United Nations votes to partition Palestine into Jewish and Arab states.
May 14, 1948	The state of Israel declares its independence and is immediately attacked by its Arab neighbors.
1951	Assassination of King Abdullah I of Jordan, the only Arab leader who had been willing to entertain discussing a peace treaty with Israel.
June 5, 1967	Israel launches a preemptive strike against the Arab armies amassing on its borders; in six days Israel defeats the Arab armies, conquering the Old City of Jerusalem, the West Bank, the Sinai, and the Golan Heights.

1973   Arab armies launch a surprise attack on Israel on Yom Kippur, the holiest day of the Jewish year.

November 1975   The United Nations adopts Resolution 3379, equating Zionism with racism.

November 19, 1977   The Egyptian president Anwar Sadat visits Israel.

September 1978   Camp David Accords signed by Begin and Sadat; Israel returns the Sinai to Egypt in exchange for Egypt's signing a peace treaty.

1987–90   First Intifada, in which Palestinians attack Israelis repeatedly with rocks and more dangerous weapons.

September 1993   Signing of the Oslo Accords by Prime Minister Yitzhak Rabin and Palestinian leader Yasser Arafat; the Oslo Accords provide a blueprint for the creation of an autonomous Palestinian region within Israel.

September 2000   The beginning of the Second Intifada, or Palestinian uprising.

ACKNOWLEDGMENTS

I feel I have been writing this book all my life, and owe thanks to everyone who crossed my path for the experience that is distilled in it. My husband, my parents and children, my family and friends, my teachers and colleagues, in discussions and arguments through the years, helped me figure out whatever I've learned about the relation of Jews to power. The sources cited cannot adequately convey my debt to the emerging field of Jewish studies, especially to its historians, and most especially to my friends among them. It also helps to have been born in east-central Europe in 1936.

When this book was included in the Nextbook series, I was fortunate to acquire the editorial oversight of Jonathan Rosen, who advised and encouraged me at every stage. He is responsible for such elegance as it may have. Dan Frank suggested further improvements. I am very grateful for help in some of my research to Jonathan Gribetz and for specific suggestions to Alex Safian, Yossi Prager, Steven Pinker, Jay Harris, Bernard Septimus, William Novak, and my brother, David G. Roskies. Errors are mine alone.

This book was written during a fruitful period in our family life. As ever, I thank my generous and noble husband, Len, and our children for the happiness they are finding in life, Abby with Ben Schachter, Jacob with Rebecca Lieberman, and Billy with Suzanne Jack. I am joyfully grateful to them and to our extended family.

The genesis of this book was the Zalman C. Bernstein Memorial Lecture in Jewish Political Thought, which I delivered in Jerusalem on January 20, 2000. I thank Hillel Halkin with all my heart for his response to the paper and Dan Polisar and the editors of *Azure*, where it appeared the following winter, for helping me hone its argument. Arthur Fried and Mem Bernstein have blessed me with their friendship and with the resources to get this book published. I am inexpressibly in their debt. The loss of Zalman was a terrible blow to Mem, to all of us, and to the Jewish people: He had the courage to become a Jewish leader, redefining for our time what it meant to reawaken Jews to their mission. His legacy survives through Avi Chai, the foundation he established to carry on his work. I hope that this book would have won his—always critical—approval.

This book is dedicated to Neal Kozodoy, who published my work in *Commentary* with the exacting generosity that makes him a legend among editors. From the age of twenty I dreamed of writing for *Commentary*, at age forty I began writing for *Commentary*, and no other literary ambition has ever superceded it. The process through which Norman Podhoretz and Neal produced the most influential magazine in Jewish history exemplifies what I know can be achieved in America. Neal reformulates in every issue the ideal of justice sustained by grace and truth. I thank him as reader, contributor, and friend.

INDEX

Index

Index

Index

Index